Jan.

TORCH BIBLE COMMENTARIES

EXODUS

C000163305

EXODUS

G. HENTON DAVIES

SCM PRESS LTD

© G. Henton Davies 1967

All rights reserved. No part of this publication may be reproduced, stored in a
retrieval system, or transmitted, in any
form or by any means, electronic, mechan-
ical, photocopying, recording or otherwise,
without the prior permission of the pub-
lisher, SCM Press Ltd.

334 00393 8

First published 1967
by SCM Press Ltd
26–30 Tottenham Road London N1
Fifth impression 1983

Printed in Great Britain by
Fletcher & Son Ltd, Norwich

CONTENTS

INTRODUCTION

COMMENTARY

From the death of Joseph (1.6) to the first day of the
second year of the Exodus (40.17)

I

THE EXODUS FROM EGYPT

1.1-15.21

CONTENTS

PREFACE

This book has been written in the conviction that after all Moses himself is the best explanation of the Book of Exodus. This does not mean that he is its author, or that there is no secondary or later material, but without Moses there could have been no such book. Behind and yet through the book is the testimony to the experience, the thinking and the convictions of this great man. The later material was only added because it was in harmony with the theme basic to Moses and to his memory in ancient Israel. The religious cast of the book points to the great age of most of its traditions, for its contents are not sufficiently 'secular' to bring them far down in the story of Israel's literature.

The author of this work recognizes that a statement so general as the foregoing must create for many people more problems than it hopes to solve, but he believes in the Mosaic basis of the book, even if it is also a mosaic with parts from several ages. The second section of the Introduction attempts to summarize recent critical study of the book for the benefit of students and others interested in that aspect of knowledge.

By an explicit arrangement with the SCM Press this book has been deliberately delayed for a number of years. Nevertheless, owing to other commitments and to all the new duties at this College, the delay has been longer than was intended. An expression of gratitude is thus due to the SCM Press for their patience and sympathetic understanding in this connection.

It remains for me to add my appreciation to Professor J. I. Durham of Southeastern Seminary, Wake Forest, N.C., and the Rev. E. W. Heaton, Chaplain of St John's College, Oxford, who have both read the manuscript and made valuable suggestions. I wish also to thank Miss E. Jones and Mrs M. Phillips, College Secretaries in succession, who have done valiantly with the typing. I am especially indebted to my wife for her help with the manuscript and with the proof-reading, and to Miss Jean Cunningham of the SCM Press for her work in preparing the manuscript for publication.

G. HENTON DAVIES

Broadhaven
Pembrokeshire

ABBREVIATIONS

AV   The Authorized Version of the Bible
EVV   English Versions of the Bible
LXX   The Septuagint, the Greek Version of the Bible
NT   New Testament
OT   Old Testament
RSV   The (American) Revised Standard Version of the
               Bible
RV   The Revised Version of the Bible

NOTE

The Commentary is based on the Revised Standard Version
of the Bible.

BIBLIOGRAPHY

Some useful books for further reading.

W. F. Albright, 'From the Patriarchs to Moses', *Biblical Archaeologist* 36, 1973, pp. 5–33 and 48–76, and the books cited there.

B. F. C. Atkinson, 'Exodus' in *The Pocket Commentary on the Bible*, parts 6 ff., publ. by H. E. Walter, Worthing, 1955 ff.

D. M. Beegle, *Moses, the Servant of Yahweh*, Eerdmans, Grand Rapids, Michigan, 1972

W. H. Bennett, *Exodus* (Century Bible), 1908

W. Beyerlin, *Origins and History of the Oldest Sinaitic Traditions*, Eng. trs., Blackwell, Oxford, 1965

R. E. Clements, *Exodus* (Cambridge Bible Commentary), 1972

B. Couroyer, *L'Exode* (La Sainte Bible . . . de Jérusalem), 2nd ed., Paris, 1958

D. Daube, *The Exodus Pattern in the Bible* (All Souls Studies 2), Faber and Faber, 1963

S. R. Driver, *Exodus* (Cambridge Bible), 1911

G. Fohrer, *Überlieferung und Geschichte des Exodus*, Töpelmann, Berlin, 1964

S. Herrmann, *Israel in Egypt* (Studies in Biblical Theology 2.27), SCM Press, 1973

D. R. Hillers, *Covenant: the History of a Biblical Idea*, Johns Hopkins Press, Baltimore, 1969

J. P. Hyatt, *Exodus* (New Century Bible), Oliphants, 1971

J. P. Lange, *Commentary on the Holy Scriptures:* Vol. II, *Exodus and Leviticus*, Eng. trs., Edinburgh, 1876

A. Maclaren, *Expositions of Holy Scripture: Exodus, Leviticus and Numbers*, Hodder and Stoughton, 1906

D. J. McCarthy, *Old Testament Covenant*, Blackwell, 1972

A. H. McNeile, *The Book of Exodus* (Westminster Commentaries), 2nd ed., 1917

G. E. Mendenhall, *Law and Covenant in Israel and the Ancient Near East* (pamphlet), Pittsburgh, 1955

B. D. Napier, *Exodus* (Layman's Bible Commentaries), SCM Press, 1963

New Bible Dictionary (articles: 'Exodus' and 'Book of Exodus'), IVF, 1962

M. Newman, *The People of the Covenant*, Abingdon Press, New York, 1962

E. Nielsen, *The Ten Commandments in New Perspective* (Studies in Biblical Theology 2.7), SCM Press, 1968

C. R. North, 'Pentateuchal Criticism' in *The Old Testament and Modern Study*, ed. H. H. Rowley, Clarendon Press, 1951

M. Noth, *Exodus: A Commentary*, Eng. trs. (Old Testament Library), SCM Press, 1962

J. Pedersen, *Israel*, Vols. I-II, Oxford University Press, 1926; Vols. III-IV, 1947; see especially Vol. IV Appendix 1

C. F. Pfeiffer, *Egypt and the Exodus*, Baker Book House, Grand Rapids, Michigan, 1964

A. Phillips, *Ancient Israel's Criminal Law*, Blackwell, 1970

W. J. Phythian-Adams, *The Call of Israel*, Oxford University Press, 1934

—, *The People and the Presence*, Oxford University Press, 1942

J. R. Porter, *Moses and Monarchy*, Blackwell, Oxford, 1963

G. von Rad, *The Problem of the Hexateuch and Other Essays*, Eng. trs., Oliver and Boyd, Edinburgh, 1966

H. H. Rowley, *From Joseph to Joshua* (Schweich Lectures for 1948), Oxford University Press, 1950

J. C. Rylaarsdam, 'The Book of Exodus', *Interpreter's Bible*, Vol. I, Abingdon-Cokesbury, 1952

H. Schmid, *Mose: Überlieferung und Geschichte*, Töpelmann, Berlin, 1968

J. B. Segal, *The Hebrew Passover*, Oxford University Press, 1963

J. J. Stamm and E. Andrew, *The Ten Commandments in Recent Research* (Studies in Biblical Theology 2.2), SCM Press 1967

H. C. Trumbull, *The Blood Covenant*, Edinburgh, 1887

—, *The Threshold Covenant*, Edinburgh, 1896

H. Wildberger, *Jahwes Eigentumsvolk*, Zwingli Verlag, Zurich, 1960

Readers who would like to undertake further study are recommended to the list of books in the following articles:

G. W. Anderson, 'Some Aspects of the Uppsala School of Old Testament Study', *Harvard Theological Review* 43, 1950, pp. 239-56

J. A. Emerton, 'Commentaries on Exodus', *Theology* 66, 1963, pp. 453-56.

INTRODUCTION

WHAT IS IN THE BOOK

Soldiers say that time spent on reconnaissance during military operations is never wasted: neither it may be claimed, is space in reviewing the contents of a book.

In the Hebrew Bible the book is named after its two opening words, translated as 'and these are the Names', briefly 'Names'. The Septuagint, the Greek translation of the Old Testament, gave the name, 'Outgoing' or 'Departure' to the book, and the Vulgate, the Latin translation, followed suit with 'Exodus'. Such a title refers strictly, of course, to the contents of the first fifteen chapters only. The Authorized, or King James, Version (1611) describes the book as 'The Second Book of Moses, Called Exodus', and the Revised Version (1885) suggests the changing view of the book by inserting the word 'commonly' before 'Called'. The RV is followed in this by the American Revised Standard Version (1952). These latter descriptions are of course not original to the Hebrew Bible.

The Hebrew title, 'and these are the names', refers to the list of names given in the first chapter, the names, that is, of Jacob's twelve sons and their households who went down into Egypt. These names connect Exodus with Genesis, identifying the Israel in Egypt with the descendants of the patriarchs and introducing those who are to be delivered from Egypt. The references to 'a new king' and to the 'store cities, Pithom and Raamses', explain the bondage and labour inflicted upon the Israelites, and also raise problems connected with the date of the Exodus.

17

Ch. 2 introduces Moses the agent of the deliverance, and tells the story of his birth and concealment, of his flight to Midian and his marriage there to Zipporah.

Ch. 3 brings the reader into the Presence of Yahweh, the author of the deliverance, the God of the fathers and of the bush. Now Moses is called, commissioned and receives the assurance of Yahweh's Presence, and, later, his objections overcome, he returns to Egypt. After a mishap on the way, he meets Aaron, and they summon an assembly of the elders and the people. Their first request to Pharaoh that Israel may depart to the wilderness to hold there a feast to Yahweh is refused, and Moses, blamed by the people for the increase of their sufferings, seeks fresh instructions from Yahweh. In 6.2-7.13 Moses is said to receive another revelation of the God who has called him, and to be confirmed in his commission. This story of the further revelation may be the sequel of the first call at the burning bush or a parallel to it.

The encounter with Pharaoh is renewed, and the long and varied story of the conflict with Pharaoh and his magicians through the first nine plagues continues to ch. 11. But the infliction of plagues natural to conditions in Egypt, though 'of unexampled severity' and 'unprecedented swiftness' (Driver), fails to achieve the release of Israel, and an enraged Moses and an obstinate king part never to meet again.

Chs. 12 and 13, first focal point in the book, record the cult legend of the Passover feast and related matters, the directions for the Passover feast, for unleavened bread or cakes and for the dedication of the first-born, being twice given. What happened on the Passover night itself, and how the fleeing people journeyed first from Raamses to Succoth, and thence to Etham are related. Ch. 13 closes with the symbolic presentation of the guiding Presence of Yahweh in the pillar of cloud and the pillar of fire.

The deliverance at the Red Sea, and the destruction of Pharaoh and his host, miraculous as somehow these events must have been, prompt the thanksgiving of Moses and the dancing songs of Miriam and the women (14-15).

Seven narratives follow (16-18) recording the sweetening of the waters at Marah; the giving of the manna; the coming of the quails; the composite story of the rebellious question at Massah ('Is the LORD among us or not?'), and the striving over the 'waters of Meribah'; the victory of the aged Moses over Amalek; and, lastly, Jethro's visit to a still vigorous Moses at Sinai. Some of the events recorded in these stories may well have originally belonged to other contexts such as Num. 10, 11 and 20. The right context of the Massah story, whether here or after the events at Sinai, is less important than the emergence of the Presence theology in the rebellious question.

Ch. 19 which describes the theophany and worship, and ch. 24 the theophany and covenant at Sinai, are the second focal point in the Book of Exodus, and are really the crown of the deliverance from Egypt. Here again the Presence theme is central to the account.

The story of Yahweh, of Moses and of Israel, the story of revelation and redemption and covenant, is now not resumed until chs. 32 and 33, where the fall of Israel through the idolatry of the golden calf, followed by the breaking of the tables of the ten commandments, leads to Israel's eventual expulsion from Sinai. This crisis, as reflected in the stripping off of the festive ornaments, the pitching of the Tent of Meeting outside the camp, and the long debate between Yahweh and Moses in which Moses successfully intercedes for Israel, though not so successfully for himself, is again related to the dominant 'Presence' theme of the book. The narrative of Exodus comes to its conclusion and indeed its climax in the mysterious narratives of the parabolic action of Yahweh, who passes by and proclaims his name before Moses. This action, or 'dominical symbolism' as it may suitably be called, is the supreme illustration in the book of the

theme of the Presence, illustrating finally the religious experience and mission of Moses.

The interruptions in the sacred story (the '*Heilsgeschichte*')
have been due to certain blocks of legal material. Ch. 20
contains the ethical ten commandments with a short narrative
appendix (vv. 18-21) followed in 20.22-23.33 by what is probably the oldest legislation in the OT, namely, the 'Book of the
Covenant'. This Book is said to contain 'words', i.e. 'commands' generally in the form of the divine command or prohibition, 'thou shalt' or 'thou shalt not'; and, also, three groups
of 'judgments' relating to common law, to ceremonial worship
and to humanitarian behaviour.

Two further blocks of legal material remain to be mentioned, chs. 25-31, and 35-40. In 25-31 divine instructions are
given in great detail for the making and furnishing of the
Tabernacle, the sanctuary where Yahweh dwells, and for the
ordering of the dress and service of the priesthood. Instructions are also given for, among other things, the maintenance
of the sanctuary, the appointment of Bezalel and Oholiab to
construct the sanctuary, and for the observance of the Sabbath.
All these directions are said to be carried out in chs. 35-40,
though there are some alterations in details of the narrative.
In turn these two blocks of legal material are controlled by
the theological statement in 29.42-46 which describes the use
of the sanctuary in terms of the Presence of Yahweh. This
idea of the Presence appears to be most simply described in
such terms as 'But I will be with you' (Ex. 3.14). But such a
phrase in fact means no more than an assurance or guarantee
of success or good fortune in life or in any particular under-
taking. The true idea or experience of the Presence is given
in such phrases as 'I am the God of your father', 'I am who I
am', etc. Such phrases represent a meeting, a confrontation, at
which one of the confronting parties is believed to be God.
This is what is meant by the 'Presence' in the following pages.
A further development is seen in the phrase 'Tabernacling

Presence', which describes the belief that the 'Presence' of God was associated with an altar, or a shrine. This is expressed in such terms as 'appear before me' (23.15), or 'before the LORD' (28.30), 'that I may dwell in their midst' (25.8). (See further on 'the religious teaching of the book', pp. 46-52 below.) The idea of the Tabernacling Presence is more characteristic of legal and priestly life as illustrated in Ex. 23; 25-31 and 35-40.

This preliminary reconnaissance of the Book of Exodus thus points to the great variety of the contents, the diversity of its literary forms and the richness of its religious themes, not to mention the historical, literary and theological problems of the book. But through the rich diversity there is one theme which appears persistently throughout the book, the theme of the Presence of Yahweh. As will be seen below interpreters of the book have already conferred a rough unity on the narrative of the Exodus by the use of the term *'Heilsgeschichte'* or 'salvation-history': Professor Stein of University College, London, has suggested the use of 'Heilsgesetz', 'salvation-law', for the legal portions of the Pentateuch including Exodus. But common to both history and law in Exodus is the theme of the Presence, and it may not unfairly be claimed that this theme confers upon the diversity of the book its fundamental yet manifest unity. The book like Israel finds its origin and reveals its originality in this Presence theme.

WHAT SCHOLARS SAY ABOUT THE BOOK

In the English Versions, Exodus is described as the second book of Moses and this fairly represents orthodox Jewish, Christian and Moslem belief. The Talmud (Baba Bathra 14b) thus preserves the Jewish tradition: 'Moses wrote his own book, the section on Balaam (Num. 22-24) and Job. Joshua wrote his own book and eight verses of the Law (Deut. 34.5-12).' According to this tradition Moses wrote the Penta- teuch, the first five books of the Bible except the last eight verses of Deuteronomy which relate his death.

This tradition of the Mosaic authorship of the Pentateuch is not merely an explanation of the literary origin of these books; it is also part of the Jewish belief about the history of revelation. On this view Moses is pre-eminently the agent of Yahweh's supreme revelation to Israel, just as Mount Sinai and its covenant are pre-eminently the place and the occasion of that revelation. In retrospect how tragic it was that the modern interpretation of the OT, in being compelled to sur- render the Mosaic authorship of the Pentateuch, also felt itself obliged to abandon this view of Moses as the supreme organ of revelation in the OT.

Moses, described by Bacon as God's 'first pen', is said to be the author of certain sections—such as the Decalogue (Ex. 34.1-28), the Book of the Covenant (Ex. 24.4), the denuncia- tion of Amalek (17.14-16), the itinerary from Raamses to the plains of Moab (Num. 33.2), and the Deuteronomic Code (cf. Deut. 31.9-13, 24-6)—but any account of pentateuchal study will show the long history of the doubts and misgivings of Jewish, Roman Catholic and Protestant scholars concern- ing this tradition of Mosaic authorship. Almost 300 years have passed since a Roman Catholic priest, Richard Simon, first put forward the view that the Books of Moses are a com- pilation of many documents of various origins and dates. A century after Simon the intensive investigation of the problem of the Pentateuch began and this culminated, yet another century later, in the Graf-Wellhausen hypothesis whereby the Pentateuch is seen to be not Mosaic but rather 'a mosaic' made up of the J document (850 BC), the E document (750 BC), the Deuteronomic Code (621 BC) and the Priestly Docu- ment and Code (398 BC). Of these J, E and P are substantially represented in Exodus.

This regnant hypothesis, as it is often called, was thus not only an account of the literary origins of the Pentateuch, but also an account of the religious development of the OT. Both parts of the hypothesis, the literary and the religious, have been investigated with a thoroughness that beggars praise. There is no call in this place to review in detail the fortunes of the hypothesis, as this has already been done in Professor C. R. North's admirable essay 'Pentateuchal Criticism' in *The Old Testament and Modern Study* (1951). It is not the least of the merits of that essay that it sets forth clearly the critical history of both parts of the regnant hypothesis. In turn this shows that the rejection of the religious part of the hypothesis, namely that the religion of Israel is best understood as an evolutionary development, does not necessarily involve a similar rejection of the literary part of the hypothesis, even though, within its main features, the theory has to be modified in various ways. How then have recent developments in the critical evaluation of the Pentateuch affected the study of the Book of Exodus in particular?

The view of the Wellhausen school—the regnant hypothesis —was a theory of the first five books of the Old Testament in terms of an early period of oral traditions followed by the documents appearing at regular intervals in the course of Israel's history. This school further explained the J and E documents as the 'prophetical narratives' (S. R. Driver) of the Pentateuch, indicating by such a title that the ethical emphasis and attitudes in the Pentateuch reflected the teaching of the great prophets of the Old Testament. The prophetical point of view was read back into the pre-prophetical traditions of Israel.

It would be true to say that although several alternatives to this hypothesis have been put forward, no alternative to Wellhausen's J E D P scheme and its development commands as much support. Thus J has been divided and another source, variously named as L (lay) or K (Kenite) or S (Seir=

Edom), or N (nomadic), has been put forward. The existence
of E has been denied and affirmed. The legal and historical
portions of P have been analysed and attributed to different
origins. Other scholars have found a written document basic
and anterior to J and E, called G (from the German word
Grund) or Basic Writing.

The symbols J E D P themselves take on new meaning,
being no longer conceived as documents appearing at 850,
750, 621 and say 398 BC respectively. They have come to
represent rather complexes or streams of traditions flowing
into and eventually becoming documents. The period of oral
tradition was longer according to some, shorter according to
others. Early traditions appear in the late, and some late
traditions in the early, documents. More value may be
attached to the historical content of J E D P than was
earlier thought possible, and so a threefold or fourfold testimony to the traditions of Exodus appears. The evaluation of
J E D and P in terms of literary style, historical event and
theological idea shows the exciting variety on which the
pentateuchal unity depends.

Nevertheless major challenges to the J E D P position
have appeared. J. Pedersen announced in 1931 that he had
abandoned the J E D P hypothesis and claimed that the
narrative centre of the Pentateuch was the Passover legend
contained in Ex. 1-15, which had its origin in Israel's worship,
and had the form of a 'cultic glorification' of Israel's God in
his triumph over Egypt. The material itself contains early
elements like the Passover, royal elements from king and
Temple in the portrayal of Moses, and post-exilic elements
showing the stamp of Judaism in the features of intercession,
etc. I. Engnell of Uppsala went even further, claiming a cultic
origin and character for the material in terms of a South
Canaanite-Israelite Spring Festival. The material has since
been given the historical veneer it now bears in the OT.

Wellhausen had claimed that J E D P were documents

revealing prophetic standpoints. Pedersen and his successors speak of temple legends and liturgies revealing the myths and rituals of Israel at worship. Exodus now reflects not prophecy but temple practices and ideas.

Other scholars have gone further, abandoning the J E D P scheme, and regarding Deuteronomy, not as the conclusion of the Pentateuch, but as the introduction to the books that follow. These speak of a P Bible, Genesis to Numbers, culminating in the death of Moses which originally stood at the end of Numbers and not as at present at the end of Deuteronomy, and of a D Bible—Deuteronomy to II Kings. This view of a P Bible and a D Bible provides helpful signposts towards the understanding and interpretation of the early traditions, but does not exclude the presence of J E material as well.

M. Noth and G. von Rad serve themselves heirs to both points of view. On the one hand they maintain the symbols J E D P, but virtually accept the P and D Bibles system, claiming that basic to the Pentateuch, and to J E D P, are the credal confessions as found in Deut. 26.5b-9; 6.20-24; Josh. 24.2b-13, etc. These *Credos* exhibit stable and permanent elements in contrast to the variable re-interpreting and expansion of the credal elements in the traditions which grew out of them.

Out of the stable elements of the *Credos* have grown the five great themes of the Pentateuch: Promises to the Patriarchs; Exodus from Egypt; Revelation at Sinai; Wilderness Wanderings; Entry into Canaan. Of these the Promises to the Patriarchs and Revelation at Sinai were later additions. Moses originally belonged to the Wilderness theme only, but was later carried over into the Exodus and Sinai themes. This view of the *Credos* as the matrix of the traditions and of the Pentateuchal themes underestimates the role of the *Credos* as summaries of already existing traditions, summaries called into being by the needs of story-telling, education, worship, training in the priestly office, and the like.

Ever since 1801 Deuteronomy has been seen as the pivotal point for the understanding of the Pentateuch, and in and over Deuteronomy the pentateuchal problem will eventually be resolved. Nevertheless the battle for the Pentateuch is for the present being fought on the Book of Exodus. Does the book merely reflect prophetic teaching or cultic practices from later Israel, or does it enshrine real history and real Mosaic thinking? Is Moses the central figure of the book or only a literary importation—a nomadic nonentity, whose desert grave and Midianite wife are mentioned, elevated into the apostle of Israel's redemption? These are some of the questions around which the struggle rages at the present time.

Independently of all this and in a fresh approach D. Daube claims that legal customs and practices are at the base of the Exodus pattern and the stories and themes of the Book of Exodus. This interpretation of the book and of social and legal practices offers yet another alternative to the prophetical and cultic theories of other scholars. Such a view lends itself more easily to the narrative form of the Pentateuch.

The varying methods of critical approach have all made their contribution to the understanding of the Pentateuch in general and Exodus in particular. The higher critical or literary approach has bequeathed the symbols J E D P, and the materials in Exodus will surely continue to be interpreted in the light of these symbols. Form-criticism has shown how the contents of any given piece of literature are closely connected with its form, and how the form affects the content and *vice versa*. This kind of critical study has also helped us to understand the difference between the moment when the tradition was first born, and that later moment when the tradition was recalled out of memory, became alive again, and was then preserved in some particular way, for example by being memorized or later by being written down.

Form-criticism has its most notable fruit in the credal or confessional approach. Some of the formal units have been

recognized as short statements of belief—the *Credos*—as
listed above. These rank not merely as sentences of tradition
destined for expansion into the great themes of the Pentateuch, three of which are present in Exodus, and all five of
which are mentioned or assumed. These sentences of belief
are also the summaries of extended traditions already in
existence and pointing by their very existence to many more
and well known elements of the story.

Most fashionable of all at the present time, and especially
on the Continent where it is exemplified in the work of Wildberger, Beyerlin, Fohrer and others, is the so-called traditio-
historical approach. This approach seeks to set forth the
history of tradition, the process of growth by which a story
or a string of stories achieves its final form. Grammatical and
syntactical features, the choice of words and the style of
diction are the raw materials of the approach. All these, interpreted in the light of polemical, theological and tendentious
attitudes, shape the material until it achieves its final editing.
The comparative study of similar units is the strength of this
approach as the subjective criteria of its exponents are very
often its weakness. Hence more emphasis is laid on the
'traditio' aspect of the approach and less on the 'historical',
and so the next question about the Book of Exodus concerns
its history. How much of it is historical?

This fundamental question remains. The view adopted in
this commentary is that the basic facts shine through whatever of prophetical, liturgical or social expansions have taken
place. The 'bare facts' of the Exodus are in themselves so
basic, so powerful and so distinctive that they shine through
such cultic glorification, or transforming re-interpretation, as
they have undergone. The 'bare facts' of Exodus attracted
like a magnet further glorifying tendencies because they were
so splendid in themselves. This is especially true of the plague
traditions in Ex. 7-11.

Fundamentally Israelite in idiom and symbol, the events

and the experiences of the life of Moses and his mind are bequeathed to us in the Book of Exodus.

THE HISTORICAL BASIS OF THE BOOK OF EXODUS

C. R. North explains the pentateuchal history as 'Salvation-History' (Heilsgeschichte) and claims that 'in sacred history . . . the alleged "bare facts" are transfigured by faith until they can be almost unrecognizable' ('Pentateuchal Criticism', in *The Old Testament and Modern Study*, p. 75). Thus the fashion has been set, following Pedersen's lead, of distinguishing between the original but no longer recoverable 'bare facts' of the book, and the transforming faith, or the 'cultic glorification' of these facts. Such a distinction is largely true of the account of the plagues in chs. 7-11, where Moses' divinely controlled words and action almost automatically bring on or remove the terrible events of the plagues. Certainly the way in which the plague stories are told reflects the exquisite and poetic art of the story-teller, but the original pattern of events is not thereby lost. There was a series of physical disasters of unprecedented number and severity coincident with Israel's struggle with Pharaoh, and these events doubtless were some of the means whereby Moses brought pressure to bear on the Egyptian authorities. Further, the plagues are entirely consonant with the Nile and the Egyptian scene, concerned not with circumstances and events unfamiliar to Egypt, but with flooding, murrain and locusts, all so well known in Egypt. Nevertheless when Pharaoh, instead of seeking the immediate disappearance of the frogs, proposes in a leisurely way that they shall depart on the morrow, he shows an unreal attitude, and is obviously an exaggerated figure of fun for the story-teller.

The Book of Exodus abounds in facts which are recoverable because they are basic to faith's interpretation of the story.

Thus Moses' birth and upbringing and his Egyptian name;
the Egyptian names of members of the tribe of Levi; Moses'
family tree and the genealogies of the sons of Jacob; the description of social conditions in Goshen, in the wilderness and
at Sinai are largely historical. Semites and denizens of the
desert did enter Egypt. There was bondage; there were building operations and there was thirst on desert marches. But in
addition to these personal, family, tribal facts and those of
habitat, extraordinary and memorable events abound: murders of babies; the disasters of the plagues; the death of the
Egyptian first-born; and an extraordinary rescue operation
from the very jaws of an Egyptian army.

The distinction drawn between the bare facts and these
same facts as transformed by faith loses a good deal of its
validity when some of the 'bare facts' are also seen to be facts
of worship and cult. Two historical journeys at least are
clearly visible in the book. The first is Moses' return mission
from the desert to Egypt to organize and engineer the deliverance of his fellows. The second is the flight of this same
rescued folk from the scene of their deliverance to the safety
of the desert fastnesses, and especially to that place from
which Moses had set out. These two historical movements
receive religious interpretations. The first is seen in God's
visitation in Egypt to deliver Israel. The second is seen in the
pilgrimage to Sinai for worship and covenant. These are the
religious beliefs in which Moses accomplished his mission,
but these beliefs are not a late faith read back into Exodus
from prophets and priests of later time; they are more likely
the facts of the faith of the man Moses, and as such some of
the religious 'bare facts' of the Book of Exodus.

The two principal foci or nuclei of the book may thus be
stated. Moses' call issues in the conviction that he must go
to Egypt to effect the rescue of his people. His mission, however, only expresses the further faith that his God, Yahweh, is
the real redeemer. The Lord himself visits Egypt for this

purpose. Moses thus presents the demand for Israel's release as the Lord's demand—let my people go—and the demand finds confirmation in the disasters of the plagues. All these issues find religious expression and their fulfilment in the events of the first Mosaic celebration of the Passover feast. On this night the coming of God to Egypt finds its keenest, most dramatic and final form. The Passover is the festival of the visiting God—visiting to defeat Egypt, and to deliver his people. Passover night is the climax of the sojourn in Egypt and of the struggle with Pharaoh, and as such is the first cultic and historical nucleus of the book.

The second nucleus stands likewise at the end of Israel's journey from Egypt to Sinai. In chs. 1-15 references to the feast in the wilderness are constant and dominant, and show that these chapters cannot be a self-contained unit. Beyond Egypt lies the desert, after slavery comes freedom, after the journey is the festival. Israel, redeemed from Egypt by her visiting God, is now herself to visit that God at his mountain headquarters. There at Sinai amid theophany, law-giving and sacrifice, covenant will be made, and the beginnings of Israel constituted in the divine Presence. The covenant at Sinai is the festival of the visited God, and is the goal of the first part of the desert journey and the geographical and spiritual climax of the entire book. The festival at Sinai is the second cultic and historical nucleus in the traditions.

The two movements, the faith that inspires them and the ceremonies that express and complete them, all belong together and are the historical, religious and liturgical 'bare facts' of the book. The unity to be discovered in the two movements and the two festal occasions suggests a unity born of a master plan through which the mind of Moses was expressed. In turn the mind expresses the mission, and the mission the faith of Israel's first apostle. The unity of movement and festival are thus the Mosaic 'bare facts' of the chronicle, serving in turn the Presence theme.

Likewise the murmurings and complaints, the sins and the apostasies of these people in the book are not the imaginary blackmail of later generations; they are the sad and customary facts so far as Israelites are concerned. They belong equally to the events before and after the book's ceremonial climaxes.

The central 'bare fact' of the Book of Exodus is undoubtedly the figure of Moses, though his existence and influence have often been denied. The origins and faith of Israel demand such a figure. If he was not there, he would have to be invented. The recovery of the figure of Moses, however, has now gone much further than the recovery of a shell. The warm outlines of the life and work of the man may be more confidently filled in. He is known in his youth and age, and in the creative parts of his life; something of his temperament is presented—for he was enthusiastic, hot-tempered, yet meek. The main outlines of his plan of campaign are recognizable, recorded in the story and preserved in the liturgical occasions of the book. His teaching, prophetic, priestly and law-making activities are set forth, and what need is there to doubt these? Furthermore, evidence of the religious faith and experience of Moses is not lacking. The Book of Exodus is controlled by the theme of the Presence. God comes to Moses in his call, and the idea of this Presence appears and reappears through the stories and through the symbolic narratives punctuating the main events and the successive stages of the book. In the legal sections too the making of the sanctuary and the ark is drawn into the Book of Exodus because it serves this theme of the Presence.

The remarkable religious coherence of the book points to this conception of the Presence as the master theme of the book, not as something imported by faith from later ages, but as reflecting the experience and convictions of Moses himself. The idea of the Presence is the basis of the conviction of his call, the mainspring of his work; it causes the problem of the desert crises in 17.7, and is the measure of his hope; it ex-

plains the meaning of the symbolism of Pillar and Cloud, of
Name and Ark, and especially of the passage of the Lord
(33-34). The Presence of the Lord was Moses' primal faith
and his preaching and his message to his people. This is the
faith he sought to impart to his fellows and this faith is
reflected in the book.

THE MIRACULOUS IN EXODUS

Certain sections of the Book of Exodus abound in the
miraculous. Ch. 3 tells of the burning bush that was not
consumed; ch. 4, of the rod made serpent, and then turned
back again; of Moses' hand made diseased and then healed,
and of the prediction that Nile water could be turned into
blood. The plague narratives (chs. 7-10) describe the wonder-
working deeds of the rod, and the hand with the rod, of Moses,
and those of Aaron, and of the partially successful secret arts
of the Egyptian magicians. These narratives culminate in
chs. 11-12 in the sudden, miraculous slaughter of the Egyptian
firstborn. Ch. 14 describes how the fugitive Israelites miraculously crossed the sea, whereas the pursuing Egyptian host
was drowned in the returning waters. Later in the wandering,
water is sweetened at Marah (15.25), manna and quails are
provided for food (16), and water again at Meribah (17.1-7).
Other miraculous phenomena but of a different kind, are
present almost throughout the entire book.

All these narratives employ a terminology of the miraculous. The four principal words are (a) wonders (3.20), (b)
miracles (4.21), both of which are used exclusively in relation
to Pharaoh and Egypt; (c) signs (4.8f., 17, etc.) used in reference to Israel and Egypt; and (d) judgments (6.6, etc.) of God's
deeds in redeeming his people.

The plagues are described by three Hebrew words (cp. 9.14;
11.1; 12.12), but the principal term for the divine power is the

word 'hand', thus 'mighty hand' (3.19, etc.); 'my hand' (3.20,
etc.); 'hand of the LORD' (9.3); 'by strength of hand' (13.3,
etc.); 'thy hands' (15.17). The RSV translation 'power' represents the Hebrew 'hand' in 4.21 as does 'work' in 14.31. Other
phrases are 'outstretched arm' (6.6); 'finger of God' (8.19);
'thy right hand' (15.6, etc.); 'greatness of thy arm' (15.16); and
'my power' (9.16). Miraculous events are assumed at 8.23,
'put a division', lit. 'set a redemption', and again at 9.4; 11.7,
in 'make a distinction', and probably at 9.5 in the words 'set
a time', and in the use of the word 'diseases' in 15.26. The
climax of this description is found in 15.11,

> Who is like thee, O LORD, among the gods?
> Who is like thee, majestic in holiness,
> terrible in glorious deeds, doing wonders?

These are the stories and this the terminology which account
for the atmosphere of the Egyptian chapters of the Book of
Exodus, an atmosphere which is laden with what is wonderful,
superhuman and miraculous, an atmosphere wherein the rare
achievements of human strength and understanding are also
the acts of divine power and revelation.

The miraculous in Exodus is thus abundant but also varie-
gated, and may therefore be explained at different levels of
understanding.

The secret arts of the Egyptian magicians are frankly described on a magical level, but inevitably reduce the corresponding Israelite miracles, namely, rods changed into
serpents (7.8-13); Nile water turned into blood (7.14-24); and
the sudden visitation of frogs (8.1-7), to the same level of
interpretation. The only difference is that the Egyptian magic
is imitative, keeping up with the Israelites!—whereas the
Israelite magic is to some extent redeemed by its purpose that
'you shall know that I am the LORD' (7.17), though in turn
this is offset by the words 'how I have made sport of the
Egyptians' (10.2).

Much of the miraculous in Exodus may, of course, be described in terms of natural events. Most of the calamities of the plagues, the first nine indeed, are phenomena natural to Egypt, and a miraculous character does not necessarily belong to any of them. To describe these calamities as miracles is a heightened form of speech pointing to their severity, their concurrence and to the terror which they caused, but to deny their historicity would not be reasonable. The problem of the miraculous character of the first nine plagues does not lie in the plagues themselves, but in the description of how they are brought about, and for what purpose.

Some interpreters would say that God in order to achieve his purpose would resort to threats: 'Let my people go or else . . .', and would inflict these terrible blows upon an innocent population in order to bend the will of their monarch. Other interpreters, without denying the historicity of the plagues would deny only the validity of the description, affirming that though the Israelite writers believed that God did behave in that way, no call exists for the Christian conscience to accept such a description of the character of God. Of course if the present descriptions of the plagues are only the relics of some dramatic performance, then some explanation of the forms of the description, though not of the character of God, is forthcoming. The tenth plague will call for special consideration.

The story of these major miraculous events in Exodus may be described then as an interpretation of natural events, even if this interpretation does not at the same time exhaust their meaning. The flight of some Israelite groups from Egypt is a divine deliverance; the journey through the wilderness and protection from enemies is described in terms of a pillar of cloud and a pillar of fire, typifying divine guidance; desert provisions are found in the divinely provided manna and quails; the phenomena of mountain terrain are used to set forth a theophany; the thoughts, convictions and experiences of men's hearts are described in terms of a burning bush, of Pharaoh's divinely hardened heart, of interviews and law-givings in Sinai, and especially in the dominical symbolism of the deity in transit (33f.). In all these instances the miraculous is found in the interpretation of natural events. This interpretation is of course essentially the work of Moses whose mind is mainly reflected in the thought of the book. The supreme miracle of the book is thus Moses himself, and his interpreting ministry in the midst of a series of quite extraordinary events.

This interpretation thus affirms the supernatural in the historical event. It is written, 'Where two or three are gathered together in my name, there am I in the midst' (Matt. 18.20). These words describe a tiny group of persons gathered for Christian worship, but this is not the total meaning. There is an extra or plus of experience which is not exhausted by the description of a group of people. So the great facts of the Book of Exodus listed in the previous paragraph may bear a double description: the flight from Egypt is also a divine deliverance, and so on. Many who read and study the book today will accept this double description, but others of course will deny the supernatural evaluation.

Nevertheless when all is said and done about natural events, about Hebrew methods of description, and about theocentric interpretation, a hard core of miraculous material remains, represented by the signs in Moses' call (Ex. 4), by the rod turned into a serpent, and then back to a rod, by the healthy hand first diseased and then restored, and of course by the tenth plague, the divine slaughter of the first-born of Egypt (11f.). In terms of the miraculous these are the cruces of the book.

Moses, like so many of those called of God in the Bible, seeks to avoid his commission, adducing many reasons for his refusal. God overcomes his plea that his compatriots will not listen to him by performing there and then the signs of the rod and of the hand, and by promising a third sign if the first two

fail (4.1-9). No amount of description or interpretation can
deliver us from the blunt questions: Did God turn the rod
into a serpent? Did he make Moses' hand diseased and then
heal it? Did he or didn't he?

All believing interpreters will say that God could do these
signs, and some will say that he did, but others will say he
would not. Moses went on protesting even after experiencing
these signs!

Let us first assume that God did these signs, that he did
them in order to convince Moses that he in turn might convince the Israelites, so that the grand design of the Exodus
might be accomplished. These two unique signs then find their
justification in the unique object of the Exodus, and so both
signs and Exodus are due equally to the direct and personal
intervention of God. This is the perfectly valid reasoning of
many believers, though it is not without its difficulties.

Thus for example, how extraordinary it is that our Lord,
faced with the temptations arising out of his messianic calling,
eschewed and denied the signs proposed by the devil. The
stories of Moses and our Lord are only partially parallel, but
it is difficult to assume that signs for Moses can be right and
God-given, when in the story of our Lord, with so much more
at stake, the signs are refused and denounced. Which story
then more closely accords with the character of God? Did
God really compel the acquiescence of Moses through these
signs? The common experience of many people who are
called, even though they be far less significant mortals than
Moses, is that they have had no such signs, but have had to
depend exclusively upon the compulsion of an inner conviction, and upon that alone. Thus many believing interpreters
would claim that because the signs done for Moses are unique,
they are therefore and inevitably irrelevant, both for the
experience of our Lord in the same situation, and for the
majority of those that are called.

Many interpreters therefore believe that God did not do

these signs because God is not of such a nature as to resort to such methods. On their view the signs are to be explained as part of the spiritual doubts and travails of Moses in regard to his call, exaggerated into physical miracles.

Lastly, the tenth plague calls for consideration. If this plague originally consisted only in the death of Pharaoh's own first-born, as 4.23 would imply, then the death of Egypt's first-born would be a natural event, remarkable and effective only because it happened in the night of the spring full moon, the night of the planned flight from Egypt. The miracle is a coincidence, but the coincidence is rightly interpreted as a miracle.

But the story stands in 11.1, 4-8, and particularly 12.12, 27, etc. in very different form. The Lord passed through the land of Egypt and slew the first-born of man and beast in that land. The question of course is again not, 'Could he?' but, 'Did he? Would he?' There are those who would affirm that for his glory and the fulfilment of his purpose God did this. There are others who would claim that the God who is revealed in other parts of the OT and in the NT is of such a character that he would not do this. Scripture is alike the authority for those who affirm and those who deny the divine slaughter of the first-born.

The Book of Exodus abounds in the miraculous, because it abounds in the experience of the Presence of God (cp. Matt. 11.2-6; and Luke 7.18-23). The ordinary circumstances of life and event in the Book of Exodus have for their penumbra what is astonishing, wonderful and superhuman. In turn this penumbra is under his feet as it were a pavement of sapphire stone, like the very heaven for clearness (Ex. 24.10), the footstool of his Presence.

PROBLEMS OF THE EXODUS

The 'bare facts' of the Exodus story no doubt include stories

concerning the deliverer and the deliverance in Egypt, the
flight and freedom from the Egyptians, the sojourn at the
desert shrine and the law-giving and covenant there. In turn,
however, all these 'bare facts' contain historical problems of
varying difficulty. The first and most discussed problem is the
date of the Exodus, and that date has been variously placed
in the sixteenth (=expulsion of Hyksos from Egypt about
1580 BC), the fifteenth (chronological date), differing dates in
the thirteenth (genealogical date) and even in the twelfth centuries.

When did the Exodus take place?

The problem of the date of Israel's Exodus can only be
studied fully in the light of evidence derived from the Bible,
from non-biblical documents and inscriptions, and from
archaeological findings especially from Transjordania, Jericho
and some Palestinian cities. All this evidence has been most
fully considered by H. H. Rowley in *From Joseph to Joshua*
(The Schweich Lectures for 1948), to which the reader is
specially referred.

It will be sufficient for the present purpose to show how the
problem of the date of the Exodus emerges from within the
different parts of the biblical traditions. The problem is acute
simply because so much biblical evidence may be cited in
favour of each view. Again, it is not possible to refer to all
that biblical evidence here but rather to illustrate the problem
with a selection of the material.

Solutions of the problem which have pointed to the sixteenth
and twelfth centuries have not gained much support because
of the weakness of the biblical traditions adduced to support
them. The real issue is between the fifteenth century (chronological) date, and the thirteenth century (genealogical) date for
the Exodus.

(a) I Kings 6.1 records that the 480th year after the Exodus

coincided with the fourth year of King Solomon's reign.
Estimates of the date of Solomon's accession vary by as much
as 25 years, though it is probably to be placed between 976
and 970, so that Solomon's fourth year would be between 972
and 966. These dates with the addition of the 480 years would
yield between 1452 and 1446 as the date of the Exodus.
Numerous arguments including some datings of the fall of
Jericho and the Habiru attacks on Palestine support this view.
On this view the Exodus took place about the middle of the
fifteenth century and Thothmes III was the Pharaoh of the
oppression.

(b) Ex. 12.40 records that Israel was in Egypt for 430 years,
though the text of the Samaritan Exodus and that of the Greek
Bible have the effect of making the sojourn 215 years. Such
records of the genealogies of this period as are extant in the OT
clearly do not account for so great a figure as 430 years for
the sojourn. For example: Jacob, Levi, Kohath, Amram,
Moses and Aaron (Ex. 6.16, 18, 20); Jacob, Levi, Kohath,
Izhar, Korah (Ex. 6.16, 18, 21); Jacob, Reuben, Pallu, Eliab,
Dathan (Num. 26.5, 89). Such examples of family trees can
scarcely be said to span a period of 430 or even 215 years.
Similarly according to Ruth 4.18-22, David is the ninth
generation from Pharez, Jacob's grandson, so that Solomon
is the twelfth generation from Jacob. These twelve generations
must then equal the 430 years of the sojourn in Egypt and the
480 years from the Exodus to Solomon's fourth year. Twelve
generations for 910 years is equally most unlikely.

Ex. 1 gives the impression that no long interval elapsed
between the death of Joseph and the accession of the oppress-
ing Pharaoh, and this is also suggested by the average of four
generations to include the sojourn in Egypt and the subsequent oppression and liberation. The genealogies thus show
that in contrast to the chronological scheme which spreads
out the period from Abraham to Solomon to more than a
thousand years, the genealogies have the effect of shortening

the periods from the Exodus to Solomon, of the sojourn itself, and from Abraham to Solomon in general.

The shorter periods implied in the genealogies harmonize with Ex. 1.11 which tells of the Israelite building of the store cities of Pithom and Raamses, cities built during the reign of Pharaoh Rameses II who reigned for the first seventy years of the thirteenth century BC. On this view, then, the Pharaoh of the oppression was either Seti (Sethos) or his successor Rameses II, and the Pharaoh of the Exodus either Rameses II or his successor Merneptah. Much evidence, including some datings of the fall of Jericho, and also the fact that Moab and Edom were apparently largely unoccupied before the middle of the thirteenth century, supports this thirteenth-century date of the Exodus.

The date of the Exodus is still under debate, for there is evidence for and against both views which is difficult to rebut. The importance of the problem, however, is not merely chronological, for the date of the Exodus also points to the much larger and more important problem of the growth of Israel as a nation. According to this larger context it has become clear that some parts of Israel settled permanently in Canaan long before the Exodus (e.g. Gen. 12 and 34). It is the merit and strength of the chronological theory that it reminds us of these northern and central settlements of Israel in Canaan during the Amarna age. Also prior to the Exodus are probably the settlement and consolidation of Judah and kindred groups in southern Palestine during the Amarna age and the two centuries thereafter (e.g. Gen. 38).

It is the merit and strength of the view based on the genealogies that, starting from the store cities of Pithom and Raamses, it traces the movement of the tribes fleeing from Egypt, through the desert wanderings to the main central settlement in Canaan under Joshua.

The weight of evidence relating to this period suggests broadly that the settling of the Israelites in Canaan went on for several centuries, but prominent in that settlement are those tribes which came out from Egypt about 1230 and later settled in Palestine. The long continuing entry into Canaan includes then those who came out from Egypt with Moses and who were later led into Canaan by Joshua.

The Bible witnesses that the tribes of Israel were all of kindred stock and indeed of common ancestry. In spite of their kindred stock the various tribes yet pursued their individual ways, though in the main two principal ways may be recognized: settlement in Canaan; and exodus from Egypt, followed by settlement in Canaan. All these tribes achieved their religious and political unity under David and Solomon, even though they were soon to lose both under Solomon's successor, Rehoboam.

Who came out from Egypt?

The census of Israel in Num. 1 shows that Israel in the desert could deploy 603,550 fighting men (cp. Num. 26.51, 601,730). Taking into account an equal number of women and twice the number of children, Moses must have evacuated at least $2\frac{1}{2}$ million persons from Egypt. This figure is impossibly high, for in Egypt the Israelites had but two midwives, and the implication of the narrative is that they were expected to be present at each birth. Then again after the settlement in Canaan the tribe of Dan could deploy 600 fighting men. Such a figure would give a total of between 6,000 and 10,000 fighting men for all the tribes of Israel, were such a calculation possible.

It is likely that the Exodus from Egypt was accomplished by a few hundred, at very most a thousand or two, and even two thousand is a great multitude in such circumstances. Who then were these people?

Moses' own tribe, the tribe of Levi, was represented in Egypt. The Egyptian names of the tribe confirm that (cp.

I Sam. 1.3, etc.). Further the denial, made by some scholars, that the Joseph tribes were in Egypt is so great a reversal of the biblical story as to be scarcely credible. Joseph—Ephraim and Manasseh—and Benjamin were certainly in Egypt. It would be reasonable to suppose that some other southern tribes were also represented in Egypt, especially Simeon in view of his association with Levi (Gen. 34).

The case is more difficult in regard to Judah in view of his Canaanite connections (Gen. 38) and to the four concubine tribes, Gad and Asher, Dan and Naphtali (30.9-13 and 35.25). These are not ranked so highly in Israel as the eight tribes said to be directly descended from Jacob's two wives, Leah and Rachel. The four concubine tribes may have been counted to Israel at a time later than the original tribes. Similarly the covenant at Shechem, centre of an area not said to be con- quered during Joshua's invasion, points to the presence of Israelite elements which did not go down into Egypt.

Any claim that Asher or Gad or Judah or Reuben were not in Egypt could be modified so as to allow elements or clans from the tribes to be in Egypt, even if the bulk of any tribe had remained in Palestine. The Bible does say that all the tribes were in Egypt, and there is no reason to deny that almost all the tribes were represented by some of their mem- bers among the Israelites in Egypt. Some present-day English families really did come over with William the Conqueror in 1066, some no doubt came a little later, and some families simply say they did so come. Elements of most of the Israelite tribes, the nucleus of the future northern and southern king- doms, did come out of Egypt, but other elements in Israel claimed to come out and the Bible records that claim.

What was their destination?

The route the Israelites took depends on where they were going. Canaan was the ultimate objective but there is no doubt that Moses was to lead Israel in the first instance to the scene of his own call, to the mount of the burning bush. This mount is variously called Sinai or Horeb, and its locality is much debated.

The traditional site is some part of the present Jebel Musa in the apex of the Sinaitic peninsula, in or near what were Egyptian spheres of interest in the days of the Exodus. The age of this tradition is uncertain but the presence of St Catharine's monastery close at hand is the main piece of evidence. On the other hand the claim for Jebel Musa is stronger than that for Jebel Serbal, a mountain with five major peaks and the most striking mountain in the Peninsula, more than thirty miles north-west of Jebel Musa. The approach to and climate of this mountain do not appear to correspond to the biblical stories.

Alternatively Sinai has been placed somewhere along the eastern side of the Gulf of 'Akaba, where the land of Midian (Ex. 2.15) was located. Similarly references to the Amalekites (Ex. 17.8-16) and to Seir (Deut. 33.2, Judg. 5.4 and cf. Hab. 3.3) suggest that Sinai was near Edom, somewhere south of the Dead Sea near the northern end of the Gulf of 'Akaba. It has also been claimed that the extinct volcanoes of the eastern coast of 'Akaba accord with the volcanic picture of Sinai in Exodus, though it is likely that the volcanoes were extinct long before biblical times.

A fourth view sets Sinai in the vicinity of Kadesh, the modern Ain Qudeis about fifty miles south from Beersheba (cp. Ex. 17.7 and Num. 20.13). The wilderness of Paran, where Kadesh was situated, was either the first stopping place after Sinai (so P in Num. 10.12), or the third (so J : Num. 12.16), but Paran is some eighty miles from Jebel Musa. In the old credal recitations (cp. e.g. Deut. 26, Josh. 24 and Psalms 78, 105) Sinai traditions are absent, and the Kadesh and Sinai traditions may be competing claims. This evidence agrees with D (Deut. 1.2) and with P (Num. 33.16, 36) in separating Sinai from Kadesh by journeys of eleven days and twenty stations respectively, but suggests that the original mountain of the desert was at or near Kadesh. The D and P separation of Sinai and Kadesh are fatal to this view. The rival traditions of Sinai and Kadesh are best explained by supposing that Sinai was the home of desert Israel for but a short time, at most a year. From here they were driven out, and their headquarters in the desert, for such time as they were there, were at Kadesh. There are, however, great difficulties implicit in any explanation of these rival traditions of Sinai and Kadesh.

A fifth view which regards Sinai as a mythical home of the god may be discounted, even though mythical or symbolic features are present in the description of the mountain.

What route did they take?

After crossing the Sea of Reeds—the Red Sea—the Israelites may have made the long journey to the south-east into the peninsula of Sinai. This is substantially the account of the P document. The J writer, however, speaks of a comparatively short journey first to Kadesh and then on to Sinai. The E document is substantially the same except for the visit to Marah and Elim. The route of the journey is unimportant compared with the destination. It is unlikely that the crossing of the Sea of Reeds was at the northern end of the Gulf of 'Akaba as some have claimed, or at Lake Bardawil as others have thought. The sea which the Israelites crossed was probably not the Red Sea, but some area of water in the locality of Lake Timsah.

THE MOSAIC AGE

The Mosaic age is one of the best documented ages of the Old Testament, and this is true of both the fifteenth- and

thirteenth-century dates of the Exodus. In this commentary
the thirteenth century is presupposed and this gives the
Amarna age as the chronological hinterland for Moses and
his work.

About half a century before the birth of Moses, Ikhnaton
had embarked upon his reforms of the old Egyptian religion.
His monotheistic tendencies and reforming zeal however were
to leave no enduring institutions, in spite of the firm and
radical policy which he pursued. Further, there is no evidence
at all to connect the reforms of Ikhnaton with the religious
training of Moses or the religious convictions which the latter
formed later in his life. Nevertheless the geographical and
chronological hinterland of the days of Moses includes a
reform in Egypt which had monotheistic features for its chief
characteristic. In a hymn of surpassing beauty composed in
honour of his god, Aton, Ikhnaton says:

> O sole god, beside whom there is no other,
> Thou didst create the earth according to thy heart
> Whilst thou wast alone.

Comparable expressions are to be found in certain hymns both
before and after the Amarna Reformation of Ikhnaton.
Monotheistic tendencies were abroad in Egypt before and
during the Mosaic age.

Scholars have also drawn attention to the names of the
Indian gods, Mitra and Varuna, present in the god-list of the
treaty between Suppiluliumas the Hittite (c. 1370-1335) and
Mattiwaza the Hurrian. These gods Varuna and Mitra were
conceived as the directing powers behind other gods, and
Varuna, a holy and ethical deity, was thought of as the creator
of all things. It is a tragedy that the early promise of these
gods, and especially of Varuna, thus prominent in an early
Indo-Iranian movement, was not sustained in later religious
development. Nevertheless incipient ethical and monotheistic

tendencies are shown to be present in this god-list earlier than the Mosaic age.

The incipient ethical monotheism of Moses, even if best described as an advanced form of the worship of one god among many, is not out of place in this religious context. There is no need to suppose that there was any influence by these earlier movements, or any borrowing by Moses and Israel. The polytheistic background of the patriarchal age has only recently been investigated, and the Mosaic discovery gains greater credence in the light of its own background.

Nevertheless Ikhnaton and his god were not to influence the world, and Varuna gave way to Indra and thus lost his way in the corridors of time. One wonders why Mosaism survived. The answer is to be found in the fact that Mosaism was born of the bondage in Egypt. Just as Moses arose out of that context to set religion upon its true path, so the second Isaiah arose out of the anguish of the fall of Jerusalem and the exile of Israel, to give that same religion its penultimate pattern, and so too our Lord out of the experiences and suffering of his earthly life and death conferred the final form and content upon that religion.

The Book of Exodus affords some evidence of the suffering and indeed vicarious role of Moses (cp. e.g. 10.28; 16.2; 17.4; 18.18-23; 32.11-14, 30-34). This has led some scholars to link the figure of Moses with that of the suffering servant in Isaiah 40-55, and so with our Lord himself.

THE RELIGIOUS TEACHING OF THE BOOK

The Book of Exodus is a book of redemption, of covenant and of worship. Exodus is a book of redemption because it records how a God, Yahweh, who was no other than the living God of the Bible, and the very author of our salvation in Christ, took mercy upon a small and insignificant people who

had been turned into a slave labour force in Egypt. In response
to their petitions, and in remembrance of his covenant with
their fathers, this God intervened and after a long struggle
was able, through the agency of Moses, to deliver them from
this bondage and to conduct them to the freedom and life of
the desert.

Exodus is a book of covenant because it is the record of
God's first attempt to found and fashion a people for himself.
Gathered at Sinai, his desert centre, God and people entered
into covenant, he to become their God and Lord, they to become his people, and his chosen community in the world. The
religious character and purpose of the divinely redeemed and
created community were vested in the institution of the
covenant.

Exodus is a book of worship, because it shows that the
deliverance from Egypt was to lead to worship at Sinai. Indeed their departure from Egypt took on the aspect of a
pilgrimage feast as they drew nearer their God. The covenant
and its ritual, the golden calf and the bent that prompted it,
focus our attention upon the meaning and goal of worship.
The new arrangements that follow the golden calf incident
were concerned with the reorganization of the worship, and
the blocks of legal material in the book after ch. 24 are concerned with the future ordering of worship.

The historical and logical order of grace and faith are
clearly illustrated in this book, for the grace of election and
redemption precede the faith of vow and worship in response,
all within the overruling providence of God. Exodus is the
book of the providence of God at the beginnings of Israel.
This providence, however, is not distant and ethereal; it is
near, direct and personal. It is the providence of a God who is
personally present at all stages of the story, and who directly
intervenes at the recurring crises. It is this personal and
ruling providence which the word 'Presence' is chosen to
designate.

Accordingly the book of Exodus is above all else in the OT the book of the Presence of the Lord. This is the thesis and the theme of this commentary. Indeed this may truly be described as no other than the theme of Israel itself, for Israel's role was to be bearer of the Presence of the Lord. In Exodus we have the dawn of the theme in the mind of Israel.

The J, E and P documents, so far as these are to be found in Exodus, are a synoptic account of the glory of the Lord in the life of a newly inaugurated Israel. They afford the 'three representations of the Divine Presence in the cloud, corresponding to the three sources . . . guiding (J), protecting (P), or (E) speaking in Israel, during its journey through the wilderness' (Driver on 13.21 f.)

The constant witness of the book to the theophanic presence and the theocentric thinking and art of these writers thus suggest that the religious teaching of the book, whether it be providence or revelation or redemption, must be related to that presentation of the personal Presence of the Lord which underlies the book and bestows a unity upon it.

The very heart of this Presence theme is the solemn statement or predication: 'I am the LORD', i.e. I am Yahweh. This is the divinely proclaimed *kerygma*, the *autokerygma*, the divine self-preaching as W. Vischer has so neatly described it. J witnesses to this divine predication (10.2, cp. 9.14 and 15.3), so do E (3.14) and especially P (6.2, 6, 8, 29; 12.12; 14.4, 18, etc.). The predication is absolute, and is probably intended to be absolute. There are of course occasions when the predication is not absolute (e.g. 3.6; 8.22; 15.26; 20.2), but these are aspects of the activity of God and not the heart of the Presence. The heart of the Presence is the absolute predication, 'I am', 'I am that I am' and 'I am Yahweh.' It is not however an absolute predication spoken in isolation, an Olympic and transcendent predication, but an absolute predication spoken in relationship, in Israel. The predication is not hidden, but is a revealed predication. That is, the predication must be understood absolutely even though it is a predication in relationship. It is not necessary to the theme to enquire what the 'I am' is supposed 'to be' or 'to do'. The predication is 'I am', and the only exegesis of it is to add another 'I am'. Thus 'I am what I am.' It may be objected that this is too metaphysical a concept for Moses or the writers of Exodus. It is, however, not what they thought, nor what their conception was, that matters. The problem for the exegete is not whether Israel could think metaphysically but whether the exegete himself can experience theocentrically. What matters is the absolute form of the predication and that corresponded exactly to their experience. Moses knew from his experience that God was 'I am Yahweh.' For Moses the Lord was absolute, exclusive, total. It is consistent with this that the book should find the acme of worship or of joy, or whatever it was, not in Israel's nor in Moses' invocation of the divine name, but in the dominical symbolism of Yahweh calling 'with' or 'upon' his own name (34.6, Ps. 115.1). In this divine self-predication and self-invocation are the original exemplars of the content and form of Israel's theocentric understanding, of prophecy and the art of worship. In turn this self-predication is the clue to the various forms of predication in Leviticus, Second Isaiah, Ezekiel and the Fourth Gospel, in all of which the theme of a divine Presence is also specially prominent.

In turn the Presence theme radiates through theophany to the call of Moses (ch. 3) and his life of intercession (cp. chs. 8, 9, 10 and 32f.), to the destruction of Egypt (11.4; 12.12, 23) and to the deliverance of Israel (3.8, 16; 4.31); through covenant to the founding (19.4-6; 24.1f., 9-11, 3-8), and particularizing of Israel (33.16 and cp. 8.22); and through 'dwelling' in Israel to Israel's instruction and worship (e.g. 25.8, 22; 29.4, 32, etc.; 33.7-11; 23.15, 17).

The Presence theme with its various extensions spells out the significance of God in the stories. The Presence of the Lord is in effect the kingship of the Lord in any given situation. The royal commission of the Lord is made known in the burning bush; the divine king is present in Egypt to contest Pharaoh's claim to lordship over Israel. In his control and command of natural phenomena whether to inflict calamity or to save and feed his people, the Lord of nature is present. Sinai is the seat of Israel's king whence the divine laws are proclaimed, and the covenant and justice are enacted, and to which Israel brings the worship and sacrifice due to a redeemer king. The God of Israel is King, and his activities are those of a king. His Presence is always a ruling Presence for it is the Presence of the Saviour and King of Israel.

Within the Presence theme various aspects of the events of Exodus are instructive for Christian thinking. The overall movement of the book—deliverance from Egypt, pilgrimage through the wilderness to fuller fellowship with God, and the promised entry into the land of Canaan—has become the partial pattern for the understanding of the events of Good Friday and Easter Sunday, and is basic also to the Christian experience of the believer's deliverance from sin as well as from physical evil, and of fellowship with God in newness of life.

Then there is the relevance of the covenant conception to the idea and fact of the divine community. Covenant is the *sine qua non* of the form of the people of God (19. 5f.; Jer. 31.31-34; Mark 14.24 and parallels; and cp. Ex. 34. 9f.). The teaching of Exodus is clear that when God founds or fashions a people for himself, he does this in the form of a covenant. Just as the Holy Scriptures are given under the form of the Old and New Testaments (Covenants), so the people of God is given under the form of the covenant. The covenantal community, originally founded at Sinai, ideally conceived in the new and everlasting covenants of Jeremiah and other prophets, is actually realized in our Lord at the Last Supper. Thus what holds the Bible together holds the people of God together. Covenant is the cement alike of scripture and of church.

It is no cause for wonder that the remarkable character of the Exodus traditions has influenced all parts of the Bible. These traditions have contributed to the making of the harvest liturgy in Deut. 26, and they form a frequent theme of the major prophets. For the prophets they serve to illustrate the goodness of the Lord from whom the prophets' contemporaries have turned away. The Exodus traditions find their place in the so-called historical psalms, and besides the explicit allusions to Egypt, to Moses, the covenant and the ark, there are many psalms, primarily designed for use in the cult, which indirectly refer to desert themes and to the contents and formulae of the covenant. Notably the Exodus traditions have supplied one of the main sources of material and illustration for the preaching of the Second Isaiah. Deliverance from Egypt would well nourish the theme of return from Babylon, and it is noteworthy how, for example, the divine self-predication in Exodus finds its counterpart in Isaiah 40-55.

Though Moses does not find a place in the Old Testament comparable to his position in Exodus, the figure of Moses dominates the Book of Exodus. He is the saved remnant of the babies doomed to destruction, and he is the agent of deliverance from Egypt, the leader in the desert, the administrator of justice and the mediator of covenant and law. It is he too who generally presides at the occasions of worship, mediating the Lord's revelation to Israel, and constantly making intercession for Israel to the Lord. To Moses, dynamic but yet meek, belongs the distinction of having begun to conceive the idea of a religious community, and of having taken the first steps to bring into being a people of God. His achievement was thus varied and great, but that achievement is only finally assessed in terms of his experience and understanding of the Presence theme. Moses launched Israel on her God-bearing mission.

The Book of Exodus reveals its hero in successive roles. The adopted son of the Pharaoh's daughter becomes the called of God who wrestles like all true saints with the necessity laid upon him (2-6). The spokesman of the people and the political agitator becomes the successful leader of the revolt and desert guide and warrior (7-18). The priestly judge of the people's disputes becomes the legislator of Israel's new laws, and the leader of Israel in its covenantal and worship occasions (19-24). The leader rejected for the moment becomes the intercessor and would-be martyr of his people (32-34).

This portrayal thus exhibits apostolic, prophetic, priestly and royal features. Accordingly different scholars have selected one of these features as the key to the portrayal of Moses. For some he was essentially a priest, for others a prophet, for yet others a figure set forth with royal traits. The truth is probably that we have in Moses one of those all-round persons who must rank as a genius, who by natural endowment, by the necessities of his lot or by the needs of the people he succoured, fulfilled at one time or another all the parts ascribed to him. He was a man of God, knowing the heart of men, but penetrating also to the secret of personal fellowship with God, knowing God face to face (Num. 12.1-8).

The best explanation of the versatility of Moses is also probably the best explanation of the coherence of the Book of Exodus itself—this is how it was. The faith and work of Moses are the best explanation of the book, just as the book in spite of all its accretions and expansions is the best account of Moses.

A profound imagination shows itself in the various parts of the book, so that Exodus is one of the most imaginative books in the Bible. The imaginative passages are not continuous but rather intermittent, and occur mainly at the creative and crucial moments of, and in explanation of, the theme of the story. These intermittent passages achieve great depths of symbolic insight, and in them the ultimate message of the book and the meaning of Moses are probably to be sought.

HOW WE GOT OUR BOOK OF EXODUS

Recent study of the Pentateuch has shown that J, E, D and P are not merely codes and documents which appear at certain precise points in Israel's literary history but that they are also the outcome of a long process of oral accumulation and tradition. Indeed the process may not have been entirely oral, because analogies both in the OT and outside it suggest that smaller written units may have been among the sources used by the compilers of J, E, D and P.

It is therefore possible with far greater confidence today to envisage that in the Book of Exodus there are to be found traditions which go back to Moses himself. It is of course one thing to say that the ideas, for example, of the festivals in Egypt and Sinai, or of his general plan of campaign go back to Moses, but quite another to claim that the verbatim records of such ideas and events are also Mosaic. Nevertheless genuinely Mosaic materials are probably to be found in the book. The short form of the ten commandments and such traditional phrases as 'with a mighty hand and a stretched out arm' are conceivably Mosaic. Similarly the story of the burning bush describing the call of Moses and his question concerning the Lord's name is probably best explained as Moses' own parabolic account of his commission. Again the stories of Moses' sojournings on Sinai and especially his account of the dominical symbolism of the Lord's passing by and invocation of his own name, so far from bearing the stamp of Judaism, as Pedersen claims, are more rightly understood as parables of Moses' own thought and experience conceived and taught by himself. Deutero-Isaiah himself with all his capacity was never so daring or so versed in the Presence theme as the author of Ex. 32 ff., and who else was there not merely in later Judaism but in earlier Israel itself who was capable of such a conception? The author of these parables of the Presence theme is one of the greatest if not the greatest mind of the OT, certainly the most original. Indeed the absence of comment on these parables in the OT is not proof of their lateness, but proof of their unique character. The thought of the Lord, in 33.19, invoking as distinct from making known his name, is a thought without parallel in the OT, a thought doubtless conceived by one who has no parallel in the OT, by Moses. Is it not time that scholars should be done with a hollow Moses, with a Moses who is said to have founded a nation and established a covenanted community, but apparently either left no record of his own experience and conviction, or whose experience and conviction were not worthy of transmission?

The present task is to expound these same Mosaic parables as basic to the Exodus tradition, because, briefly related as they are, daringly and uniquely conceived, springing from and in turn nourishing religious faith, they are memorable and moving literature, bearing the stamp of genius upon them.

Indeed most of the 'bare facts' which are presupposed in the Exodus narrative were of rather an extraordinary kind, and so were memorable and easily transmitted, even if liable to attract miraculous embroidery. The Israelite clans would have much to speak of during their journey to Canaan and the stories remained firmly fixed in their memories, especially as Passover time came round each spring, and as they explained to the young what the ark was, where it had come from and what its purpose was.

No doubt after the settlement in Canaan the stories like that of the ark became associated with one or more sanctuaries and the stories of the families and the people became also the sacred legends of the sanctuaries. At this stage especially, there would be added those elaborations in which the physically miraculous was emphasized. Now cultic glorification would be at work, and history, without being lost, would be re-interpreted to suit the newer needs of worship, wonder and faith. The organization of the stories round central themes, such as Moses and the liberation from Egypt, the deliverance at the Sea of Reeds, the law-giving and the ark would confirm the outlines of the tradition reaching back to desert days, and now ready for written formulation by J the prince of story tellers and others. So J was written, as may reasonably be supposed, before the division of the monarchy, and then E some time after that division, and some of the earliest traditions remained in the priestly lore of the sanctuaries to emerge centuries later in the Priestly document put forth by Ezra and his friends.

An increasing number of scholars deny the existence of the E document. To subtract priestly material from Exodus is fairly straightforward, but the material that remains cannot all be attributed to J. Whether as a separate document, or as an extended running commentary on the J material, this non-J and non-P material is sufficiently distinctive, continuous and extensive in Exodus to warrant the claim of a separate author. This triple tradition helps to confirm the 'bare facts' of the Exodus story. If the Synoptic Gospels were compiled as one book, their testimony to the events they record could be less impressive. To analyse the narrative of Exodus into its triple tradition and thereby find double and sometimes treble confirmation of the common tradition is all gain.

As is well known J and E were later combined by an editor, and either in conjunction with Deuteronomy and the Priestly writers found their context in J E D P, or, at first with the Priestly writers only, found their place in the mainly Priestly book, Genesis to Numbers, later to be supplemented by the Deuteronomic book, Deuteronomy and the 'early prophets'.

COMMENTARY

From the death of Joseph (**1.6**) to the first day
of the second year of the Exodus (**40.17**)

PART I

THE EXODUS FROM EGYPT
1.1-15.21

THE PEOPLE TO BE DELIVERED
1.1-22

THEIR IDENTITY
1.1-6

The Book of Exodus first tells the story of Israel's Exodus or departure from Egypt, and begins by identifying this Egyptian nucleus of Israel. The priestly editor chooses his own version of the connection between this story of the Exodus and the earlier story of the forefathers of Israel. The sons of Israel are the sons of Jacob (Gen. 35.10 P), who with his eleven sons and their families join Joseph in Egypt. They are seventy in number, that is excluding Dinah, Jacob's daughter (Gen. 46.8-27).

The events of v. 6 (death of Joseph and his generation) are separated from the events of v. 7 (increase of Israel) by a long, but uncertain, period of time. From v. 7 on the children of Israel are the Israelites, and it was presumably their experiences in Egypt that preserved and strengthened the community feeling of these people.

THE PROMISE
1.7

This verse shows how the divine promise to Abraham (Gen. 12.2 J; 17.6 P) and to Jacob (35.11 P) was fulfilled in the great increase of Israel's numbers. The geographical and biological link is Joseph, described in Gen. 45.5-7 as one sent on ahead to serve as *mihya* (nucleus of life), and a remnant to preserve

life. The verbs of this verse are in part the same as those of
Gen. 1.28, though the verbs expressing dominion in the Gen.
passage are omitted here because Israel's lot is to be bondage.
THE LAND is almost certainly the eastern delta region of the
Nile—Goshen (Gen. 47.4).

PHARAOH'S THREE PLANS TO CONTROL
THEIR NUMBERS

1.8-22

8-12 J.   Pharaoh dealt wisely with his immigrant population,
and made them his labour supply to forestall any revolution
within, or alliance with enemies without. Reading with the
Samaritan Text and versions, IF WAR BEFALL US, Pharaoh's
policy was normal and reasonable but harsh and tyrannical
to the Israelites. A NEW KING, or new dynasty, suggests but a
short space of time and not the period stated in Ex. 12.40.
These verses reflect historical conditions in the time of
Rameses II (c. 1290-1225), who is possibly the new king of this
passage, and who first put the Israelites to work in the store
cities of PITHOM (House of Atum: at Tell El Maskhuta or
Tell El Retabeh) and RAAMSES (House of Rameses: at Pelu-
sium, or Tanis=Avaris—biblical Zoan—Num. 13.22, or
Qantir). Both cities are in the delta region of the Nile and may
be in the Wâdī Tumilât area; Raamses was the residence of
the Pharaoh and certainly Israel's point of departure (Ex.
12.37; Num. 33.3-5). In v. 12 the Hebrew text has the
singular: 'him, the more he . . . he . . .'.

13-14 P.   A parallel and simple statement of the fact of the
oppression; house building and irrigation works.

15-22 E.   The second and third plans to control the Israel-

ites. Egypt's king commands two Hebrew midwives, Shiphrah
(Beauty) and Puah (Brightness), to slay the new-born male
children. It appears that two of them are sufficient. (cp. Num.
1.46 and Deut. 7.7). The midwives disobey the king, present
a ready excuse, and their bravery is rewarded, for God blessed
them with families. SEE THEM UPON THE BIRTHSTOOL is lit.
'view the two stones'. The meaning is either to see the Hebrew
mothers in the act of giving birth, or look upon the stones,
i.e. tell the sex of the babies. Pharaoh's third proposal (22)
may be from the J source. THE NILE: the Hebrew word, lit.
'the river', generally means Nile, frequently in J. Herodotus
said that Egypt was the gift of the Nile. HEBREW may be the
same word as 'Apiru', frequently occurring in Near Eastern
texts. Hebrew and Apiru are overlapping terms, either ethnic
or social. Hebrew as applied to Israelites conveys a nuance of
contempt.

THE AGENT OF ISRAEL'S
DELIVERANCE

2.1-25

22 verses suffice to tell the story of nearly two-thirds of the life of Moses (Ex. 7.7), namely, his birth, upbringing, manhood, marriage and exile. The fewness of the stories is an important consideration in estimating both the significance and the historical worth of the chapter.

THE BIRTH OF MOSES AND HIS ADOPTION

2.1-10

This famous story of Moses hidden in the Nile reeds has been variously interpreted as:

(*a*) the legal adoption of Moses by the princess;

(*b*) the Israelite version of a widespread story told of many heroes; how they were exposed and yet delivered. The story of Sargon of Akkad among others is often cited; Cyrus, Perseus, Romulus and Remus are other illustrations.

(*c*) the Israelite version of that legend which relates that a king is warned that a boy to be born to his daughter will some day bring about his death. Plans to prevent conception, then to slay the baby when born, all fail and eventually the grandfather is slain by his grandson. The differences in the Israelite version and the purpose which the story serves in its present context are however very significant.

1. a daughter of Levi Jochebed (cp. 6.20 P), like her husband (Amram—grandson of Levi), was of the tribe of Levi. In Gen. 34 and 49 the tribe of Levi has a secular character, and there is nothing in Ex. 2 to suggest anything different. The word Levi in its root meaning suggests attachment, or lending,

and so the word may describe a relation to God, e.g. client of
God. In Ex. 32 the faithful Levites take the place of Aaron as
priests, but in Deut. 10 they are chosen by Moses after Aaron's
death. But the Hebrew here also means 'the daughter of Levi'
(cp. Num. 26.59). Jochebed was Amram's father's sister, that
is, Kohath's sister and so Levi's daughter. The narrative
suggests that Moses was the first-born, but elsewhere we
learn of the maid Miriam who is described in v. 8 as a GIRL,
and of Aaron, three years older than Moses. It is possible
then that Miriam and Aaron were the children of Amram by
a former marriage. Moses was comely and was hidden in a
basket made from the papyrus plant and other riverside reeds
waterproofed with bitumen (probably from the Dead Sea) and
pitch. Hidden thus as a babe, Moses himself fled into hiding
when he had grown up. God often hid him in the cloud of
Sinai, and finally he was buried in an unknown grave.

4. stood   Better, stationed herself or took her stand.

5. The story shows that the Israelites were living not far from
the royal residence.

7. nurse   Lit. a woman giving suck.

9. and I will give you   The 'I' is emphatically expressed in the
Hebrew.

10. Moses . . . Because I drew him out
   The explanation of his name as 'drawing out' rests on
assonance and is popular etymology. The name, Moses, is an
Egyptian word meaning 'son' as in Egyptian royal names, like
Tutmose, etc. This story of Moses' babyhood is thus important for preserving two historical facts. Moses was an Israelite
of Levitical descent but received an Egyptian name and upbringing.
   In the context of the Book of Exodus the reason for the

recording of this story is clear. Presumably Moses is the only
baby boy to be preserved. He is thus the remnant child of his
generation, and it is this remnant child who is to be the
deliverer of his people. Deceived by the women the Egyptians
help to save Moses and thus contribute to their own eventual
undoing. It is strange how important a part water plays in
several crises in Moses' life (cp. 14.15-31; 15.23-26; 17.1-7;
Num. 20.1-13).

MOSES BEGINS HIS ASSOCIATION
WITH MIDIAN

2.11-22

Somehow Moses knew who his people were, knew too that
they were sorely oppressed and was full of compassion for them.
His compassion for his people was of course the seed-bed of
the call and commission that he was later to receive. His
compassion led also to the first in a chain of events that was
to issue in that call. One day he killed an Egyptian, possibly
one of the foremen maltreating an Israelite, and later intervened in a quarrel between two Israelites only to be taunted
as a murderer. In fear Moses resolved to flee to the desert.
His flight can only mean that he was a far less influential
figure in the court than might be supposed, and that probably
he was more closely bound to his brethren than the narrative
otherwise indicates. Moses' violence reminds us of Levi in
Gen. 49.5-7.

The stories reveal Moses as courageous, compassionate and
easily moved to anger, enthusiastic and impetuous. One wonders whether the experience gained from interfering in the
quarrel between his compatriots was a lesson both in the
understanding of the 'hubris' spirit—the Dathan-Abiram spirit
—of his compatriots (Num. 16), and in the obtaining of that

meekness for which afterwards he became renowned (Num. 12.3).

The taunts of his compatriots must not lead us to forget that Moses was known to his brethren as the man who had killed one of the hated Egyptians. Whatever his upbringing he had acted and fled as an Israelite.

Moses finds refuge and his destiny in the desert. Here at a well he meets the woman who is to be his wife, is later introduced to her father Jethro, the priest of the god of Midian, and later still is to meet with no other than the Lord himself. The scene at the well, the priest's seven daughters, the gallant stranger, the love affair are a real life story.

The purpose of these verses is quite clear. It is to connect one primal fact of the Mosaic tradition, namely, his Egyptian name and upbringing, to that other primal fact of that tradition—his connection with Midian and some of its people. M. Noth in his *History of Israel* (Eng. trs., 2nd ed., 1960, p. 135) considers two possibilities as the point of origin of the role of Moses. The first is his Egyptian name, the second is the tomb of Moses precisely located. Noth chooses the second possibility as the beginning of his traditio-historical reconstruction of the life and significance of Moses. This choice is the great divide in this scholar's work. If he had chosen the first possibility, then his reconstruction of the life of Moses and the pentateuchal traditions and the early history of Israel would have been entirely different. Moses' Egyptian name, dress, and so on are thus the Achilles' heel of his entire reconstruction.

15. Moses flees to Midian. This is probably the area east of the Gulf of 'Akaba and adjacent territory, But the Midianites were camel nomads, the first as yet known, and so would range over a considerable area. Where Moses met the Midianites is not known, just as the location of the 'Mount of God' is unknown. Nevertheless Moses appears to have fled deliberately to Midian, and this was probably because Midian

at this time contained tribal elements friendly and possibly
related to the Israelite groups in Egypt. Certainly the five
families of the Midianites living in the east, and associated
with Ishmaelites and Midianites (cp. Gen. 37), are the
descendants of Abraham's concubine Keturah (Gen. 25.1-6).
Moses fled then from one branch of Abraham's family to
another. In the Joseph stories and the early wilderness stories
Midianites are friendly, but in the later desert stories the
princes of Midian and Moab hire Balaam to curse Israel
(Num. 22 and cp. Num. 25 and Josh. 13.21). Still later Gideon
repulses Midianite attacks (Judg. 6-8; 9.17). The tradition of
the friendly association of Moses and Midian must go back
then to this time of friendship between these peoples, and
could hardly have arisen in later times. From this verse until
4.18, which relates how Moses returned to Egypt, the scene is
set in the land of Midian.

18. Reuel (Companion of God.)   Here the priest of Midian,
Moses' father-in-law, is called Reuel. In Ex. 3.1; 4.18, etc., he
is named Jethro. Num. 10.29 is ambiguous and the name of
this man could then be Hobab or Reuel (AV Raguel). Judg.
4.11 gives Hobab. Reuel in Ex. 2.18 could have arisen out of
the ambiguity of Num. 10.29.

19. An Egyptian   Having the accent or appearance or dress
of an Egyptian. The Hebrew construction expresses the
delighted surprise of the girls.

21. Zipporah   means a small bird like a sparrow or skylark.

22. Gershom   Only son of Moses in the J tradition and
ancestor of the priests of Dan (Judg. 18.30). The etymology,
A SOJOURNER, is again based on assonance, for the root could
mean expel, or sprout.

THE COVENANT WITH THE FATHERS

2.23-25

(V. 23a J; vv. 23b-25 P.)

The Pharaoh of the oppression, Rameses II, dies and MANY
DAYS could refer to his long reign of more than sixty years.
This obituary notice serves to introduce the main theme, not
merely the agony of Israel in Egypt, but the covenant with
the fathers so basic to the Priestly writers. God remembers,
i.e. puts into operation, the covenant with the patriarchs. As
the White Queen said in *Through the Looking Glass*, 'It's a
poor sort of memory that only works backwards.'

25. knew   Took knowledge of; LXX: 'made himself known
to them'.

The stage is set, the various actors including Moses have
made their bow, and it is time for the principal personage, no
other than the Author of the deliverance himself, to appear.

THE AUTHOR OF ISRAEL'S DELIVERANCE

3.1-22

This passage is mainly J with E in vv. 1, 4, 6, 9-15, 19-22.

This chapter describing the call and commission of Moses resembles many other passages in the Bible which describe how patriarchs, judges, prophets and apostles enter the service of God. These passages exhibit common features: the scene of the action; the God who calls; the person called; his commission; the people to whom he is sent. But within each feature there is a wide and rich variety of facts and ideas well worthy of study by comparison.

THE CALL OF MOSES

3.1-10

When Moses was 80 (7.7), he happened to take his father-in-law's sheep to a western (back) i.e. more fertile, area of the wilderness where, like Jacob (Gen. 28.16), he stumbled upon a sacred site. The area is not identifiable, and the references to the mountain and to Horeb do not help very much. Horeb (ED) is possibly a part of the Sinai (JP) mountains, though this is supposition. Moses met God at a mountain in the wilderness within the area of Midian. The sudden attraction was a brilliantly illuminated bush which appeared to be on fire. ANGEL OF THE LORD, and 'God OF the fathers' are of course simply variants. The God of the fathers is making himself known to one of their descendants (E) and announcing his intention to deliver his people from Egypt.

7. my people This is the first reference to the people in this

chapter, but from now on every verse of this chapter refers
to them in some way or other. They are God's real concern.
MILK AND HONEY: the classical description—honey meaning
not only bee honey, but also *dibs*—grape juice boiled to a
syrup. PLACE OF various peoples—the verse well describes the
mixture of population present in Canaan. CANAANITES:
Semites living in the coastland of Syria and Palestine and
spreading (Gen. 10.18) over the whole of those lands.
HITTITES (see Josh. 1.4): generally the great power of Asia
Minor with control over Syria, and particularly an ethnic
group occupying parts of the Judean hills in and around Jerusalem, Bethelehem and especially Hebron. AMORITES: pre-
Israelite settlers in Canaan and living in wide areas both sides
of the Jordan. PERIZZITES: dwellers in Canaan who may have
been fellahin-peasantry—hill people, villagers. HIVITES: early
inhabitants in the land in the Lebanon, Hermon and Shechem
areas (Gen. 10.17; 34.2; Josh. 11.3, etc.), but otherwise unknown. JEBUSITES: Jebus is Jerusalem (Judg. 19.10f. etc.),
and the Jebusites are a small community centred on that city
(Gen. 10:16; 15.21f. etc.).

10. send you Here is the apostolic or prophetic commission
of Moses. There is no clash between 7f., 16f., I HAVE COME
DOWN TO DELIVER THEM (J), and 10, THAT YOU (Moses) MAY
BRING FORTH MY PEOPLE (E). The distinction preserves the
thought that the Lord is the author of the deliverance, but
as may be observed so often in the Exodus stories, e.g. in the
plague stories, what God proposes is carried out in actual
fact by Moses or even Aaron.

MOSES' FIRST OBJECTION

3.11-12 E

In the remainder of ch. 3 and in ch. 4 Moses presents four

objections against his acceptance of the task of deliverance.
The first two from E are concerned with the Presence and
Name of God, and so they rightly belong to the theme of ch. 3,
which is 'The Author of the Deliverance'. The second two,
from J, which occur in ch. 4, are concerned with the creden-
tials and capacities of Moses. The objections clearly presuppose that Moses is now an older and much more cautious
man.

Moses like David (II Sam. 7.18; I Chron. 29.14, etc.) in the
words WHO AM I? expresses not merely modesty but plumbs
the depths of genuine humility in the Presence of God. It is
the sense of God's Presence that creates this feeling in the soul
of man and it is only the sense of that Presence which cures
the condition: BUT I WILL BE WITH YOU. Verse 12 thus brings
us to one of the central doctrines of the Book of Exodus, the
Presence of God with Moses and with Israel. M. Noth's
exegesis of v. 12 is not very convincing. He assumes that it
is incomplete, is transmitted in the wrong order, and that its
SIGN is not mentioned. On the contrary! At the mountain
God assures Moses of his Presence. In the strength of that
assurance Moses is to perform his apostolic office and 'fetch'
Israel from Egypt, and the vindication of these things is that
Moses·and his compatriots will together worship God at the
place where God is now speaking to Moses. The SIGN is of
course prophetic and relates to the divine interpretation of the
events that are to happen. So the people to be rescued, Moses
in his work of deliverance, and the plan for the whole affair,
have a further, deeper meaning. It is all the work of God, but
this will not be known or proved until Moses and his compatriots are back at the place where Moses is now standing.
Then it will be seen that this people is to be the people of
God; this man Moses fulfils an apostolic mission initiated by
God, and the plan is a divine purpose, having the form of a
journey to Egypt, and a pilgrimage to the mount, and the
secret at each point is the dwelling of God with his people.

The SIGN is not merely worship at the mount, but the recognition of the Presence of God in Israel at the mount. In the SIGN cohere the first three themes of the book: the people, the agent and the Author of the deliverance. SIGN really means proof, and the proof of Moses' divine commission is an Israel rescued from Egypt worshipping God at the mount. So Moses must believe, and must wait until he gets back to this mount.

MOSES' SECOND OBJECTION

3.13-15 E

Moses is prepared to trust, but would like to know the NAME of the God who is sending him, especially in order to tell and convince the people. The name is I AM WHO I AM. To discuss these words in terms of the divine name YHWH, which they closely resemble in Hebrew, raises many difficult problems. For example, the original form of the name (the long form YHWH, the short form YHW, etc.), the original character of the name (ejaculation, descriptive verb, etc.), the root of the Hebrew verb—on all these questions numerous suggestions have been made, and the consideration of them falls outside the scope of the exegesis of this passage in this commentary. To discuss these words however in the light of their context shows:

(a) Moses' knowledge of the divine name will help to guarantee the authenticity of his mission.

(b) The first part of v. 14 is the only passage in the OT which offers an explanation of the meaning of the divine name.

(c) The meaning given explains the name in terms of the Hebrew verb 'to be'.

(d) This being is not 'pure being', as M. Noth so rightly

points out, but 'active being', a manifested being. (See his Commentary, *Exodus*, p. 45.) As Buber and others have pointed out, the Presence of God underlies the active sense of being in this passage.

(e) The words 'I AM WHO I AM', which are of the same type as 'I will have mercy on whom I will have mercy' (33.19, and cp. 4.13; 16.23; I Sam. 23.13, etc.), and could be translated as I WILL BE WHAT I WILL BE, convey a sense of indefiniteness or even of mystery. Some have taken the words to mean 'Mind your own business; I am not telling you my name,' but this is to negate the sense of mystery. More likely the words have the quite practical meaning I AM *who and what, and where and when, and how and even why you will discover* I AM. I am what you will discover me to be.

(f) The original form of the passage is difficult to discover because the divine speech is introduced three times in vv. 14f. V. 14 is divisible but v. 15 is not. V. 14a may be the answer to the first question of v. 13, and 14b the answer to the second, but there may be one if not two further answers in v. 15. Vv. 13-15 clearly belong together.

THE WILDERNESS PILGRIMAGE

3.16-18 J

The Lord has made his reconnaissance, and so is in possession of the facts. He has commissioned Moses, and now proclaims, in the form of a proposal to hold a pilgrimage feast in the wilderness, that operation Exodus is about to be carried out. This proposal may have been intended to deceive Pharaoh, to test his attitude or to represent the people in the most favourable light. The pilgrimage feast is a recurrent feature of the J Document.

EGYPTIAN JEWELLERY AND RAIMENT

3.19-22 E

The king of Egypt, it is predicted, will not release Israel, not even after A MIGHTY HAND, i.e., not when severely afflicted. The reference appears to be to the non-success of the first nine plagues. RSV follows LXX and Vulgate and reads 'unless compelled by a mighty hand'. This anticipates the plagues, but the Hebrew assumes that they will not be effective. Later, for a reason not specified, Israel will be released and will take away with them the good will of the Egyptians in the form of some of their valuables in jewellery and raiment. The request for jewellery, etc., here predicted, is not actually made until 11.2, and is actually granted in 12.35ff. This long gap may well afford a clue to the structure of the book and to the events it describes.

CONSEQUENCES OF THE CALL OF MOSES

4.1-31

FURTHER OBJECTIONS FROM MOSES

4.1-16 J, 17 E

The first sixteen verses are J's continuation of the account of the call of Moses, in which further objections are made by Moses to his commission. In ch. 3 the objections are met by assurances in oracular style (e.g. 3.12, 14ff.); here the first objection is met by three miraculous signs. If THEY, i.e., the Israelites, will not believe Moses—and there is no record of a revelation from God since the days of Jacob, nearly 430 years ago according to Ex. 12.40!—then he is rehearsed in two signs which he must perform before them: the shepherd's crook turned into a snake, and his own hand made leprous and then healed. Moses is even bidden to take the snake by the tail. This is the most dangerous part of a snake to seize, but presumably the idea is to heighten the miraculous element. If Israel will not believe this sign when they see it performed, then they will believe the second sign—his hand afflicted with leprosy (if it was leprosy) and then healed again. The magical element in these verses is very pronounced and compares unfavourably with the spiritual authority of the utterances of ch. 3. In the outcome in 7.8-12 Aaron performs the sign of the staff before Pharaoh's court and not before the Israelites, but in 4.30 (J) Aaron does the speaking and signs before the people. In 4.17 the rod is to be the instrument of more than one sign. A third sign mentioned in v. 9 eventually becomes the first plague (7.14-25).

These miraculous signs in vv. 1-9 fail to convince Moses,

and in v. 10 he now protests his lack of eloquence. God promises his help, but then Moses in 13, by an oblique utterance,
refuses. RSV (SEND, I PRAY, SOME OTHER PERSON) rightly
interprets EVV SEND, I PRAY THEE BY THE HAND THOU WILT
SEND. Moses' flat refusal occasions the Lord's wrath, but also
yields the proposal that Aaron, who is an excellent speaker,
shall be Moses' spokesman. Moses will be to Aaron as God
is to his prophets. In v. 11 SEEING, i.e. understanding, as the only
word not expressing a bodily defect, perhaps ought to be read
as 'lame' (adjectival like the other Hebrew words of the verse).
On the other hand, the pairs of words may express a totality
of human conditions and not be literally meant. The ROD (17)
will be used in connection with the plagues, the crossing of
the sea, to obtain water from a rock and in the battle with
Amalek.

LEVITE is not ethnic but a professional term for special functions, which possibly even Moses may not share.

MOSES RETURNS TO EGYPT

4.18-26

18, 20b, E; 19, 20a, 21-23 J. 18 and 19 are probably
variants. 18 records the family farewell, and does not necessarily imply that Moses departed alone. Perhaps 19 and most
of 20 once followed 2.23a. At God's command Moses takes
his family and returns to Egypt. Only one son has been
mentioned so far (2.22). No doubt the wife and two sons rode
upon an ass.

MIRACLES of v. 21a refer to those mentioned in v. 17. HARDEN,
lit. make strong. Three different Hebrew verbs are used to
describe this process of hardening. (See below on 9.8-12)
Vv. 22f. J contrast Pharaoh's first-born son with Yahweh's
FIRST-BORN SON, Israel. The word FIRST-BORN is used of
Ephraim (Jer. 31.9, etc.) and of the Davidic king (Ps. 89.27).

The first-born theme does not reappear until Ex. 11.4. Many
commentators therefore suggest that 4.22f. once stood before
either 10.28 or 11.4 and formed the introduction to the tenth
and last plague. The jewellery theme of 3.21f. also does not
appear again until 11.2-3. Instead of removing 4.22f. to ch. 11,
it would be better to assume that the sequence of the narratives is from 4 to 11, and that in chs. 5-10 we have a series of
parentheses. The FIRST-BORN of 4.22f. is Pharaoh's FIRST-
BORN only, but in 11.4f. all the FIRST-BORN of the land of
Egypt, human and animal. On the basis of 4.22f. it is possible
that the original tragedy was confined to the death of
Pharaoh's FIRST-BORN.

24-26 J. On the way to Egypt Moses fell dangerously ill.
Zipporah concluded that the illness was due to the fact that
neither her husband nor her son were circumcised. So she
circumcised her son, and then touched Moses' foreskin (lit.
FEET) with the boy's foreskin. Moses was obviously too ill to
be circumcised: so the frantic woman conceived this idea of
a vicarious circumcision. It worked too, for Moses recovered.
BRIDEGROOM OF BLOOD is reproachful, and shows Zipporah's
reaction to the emergency and makes plain that their marriage
was still fairly recent, and that she now regarded Moses as a
proper husband, even although he had only been symbolically
circumcised. The mention of FLINT suggests antiquity or desert
conditions. The necessity of circumcision is the real point of
the story, and not when it should be performed or upon whom.
Contrast SONS (20) with SON (25). In 18.2b the wife and sons
are back with Jethro. (Cp. H. Kosmala, 'The Bloody Husband',
Vetus Testamentum 12, 1962, pp. 14-28; J. Morgenstern,
'The Bloody Husband (?) Once Again', *Hebrew Union
College Annual* 34, 1963, pp. 35-70.)

ISRAEL HEARS THE GOOD NEWS

4.27-31

Moses and Aaron meet by divine suggestion. There is some disorder in the narrative. In v. 24 Moses is on the way back to Egypt; in v. 27 the brothers meet at the mount in the wilderness which Moses had left in 4.18. It is generally thought that vv. 27f. belong to E and 29-31 to J, and that the figure of Aaron is secondary. Be that as it may, Moses tutors Aaron and Aaron speaks and perfoms the signs. HEARD (31): LXX 'rejoiced', which is probably better.

THE STRUGGLE WITH PHARAOH BEGINS

5.1-6.1

This section which contains J material, except for E passages in vv. 1, 2 and 4, is notable for the presence of MOSES AND AARON in vv. 1-2, 4 and possibly in 3, for their absence from 6-19, and for their return in 20ff. These facts lead M. Noth to suppose that this chapter contains the tradition of the bondage in Egypt in its original form, i.e. without a Moses, with Israelite leaders in contest with Pharaoh, and with the Israelite claim to have received a revelation from God in Egypt resulting in their desire to hold a pilgrimage feast to their god. (See his Commentary, pp. 53ff.) But THEY in v. 3 and YOU in v. 5 probably refer to Moses and Aaron, and the revelation and pilgrimage feast are almost certainly those of the call of Moses in 3.12, and not separate events in Egypt. Furthermore, in vv. 6-14 Moses and Aaron can have no possible part to play, and really all there is to explain is the independent role of the officers in Israel, vv. 15-19. The Israelite deputation in these verses could well have taken place before the brothers returned to Egypt, or, at their suggestion and quite deliberately, apart from them. Perhaps some of the material in this section, e.g., vv. 15-19, belongs in some position after the first chapter.

The appearance of the brothers, at the beginning and end of the chapter, would be the next logical step in the development of the story. Vv. 6-14 describes what is quite a reasonable reaction on the Egyptian side, vv. 15-19 a separate plea to Pharaoh, and the remainder of the section the outcome of all these events. More difficult to explain is the fact that the Israelites have such easy and direct access to Pharaoh, but that is surely due to the compressed and simplified form of the narrative (see McNeile *ad loc.*).

MOSES AND AARON request the release of the Israelites for a
pilgrimage feast in the wilderness in the name of their God.
THE LORD, THE GOD OF ISRAEL only here and 32.27 (E) in the
Pentateuch. THE GOD OF THE HEBREWS are words correctly
used since they are addressed to Pharaoh. Pharaoh who wor-
ships the great gods of Egypt cannot even recognize such a
request. The struggle with Pharaoh begins with his absolute
refusal, and Pharaoh's attitude now becomes the central theme
until the Israelites eventually depart.

5. This must be what Pharaoh thought and realized, for he
would hardly have told his subject slaves that they were more
numerous than his own people. To say this to them would
have been to suggest a possible rebellion based on their
superior numbers.

6. THE TASKMASTERS are of course Egyptians, but the foremen
are the Israelite officers or overseers. LXX has 'scribes',
people who kept the accounts. Presumably the taskmasters
dealt with the foremen and the foremen with the workers.
Either some Israelites were now deputed to gather straw, and
the brick-makers were fewer, so that they had to work harder
and longer to make the same number of bricks, or else the
Israelites had less time for brick-making because they were
also finding straw—chopped bits of straw—to reinforce the
mud bricks, or to cover and separate the bricks in the
making. The LXX reads different verbs: 'may attend' for
MAY LABOUR in v. 9, and 'were urgent' for WENT OUT in v. 10.

13. your daily task Lit. the matter of a day in its day.

16. the fault is in your own people This represents some difficult, perhaps untranslatable, Hebrew. The Hebrew could be
read as (a) but the fault is with thee (so Symmachus, a Greek
version); or (b) thou shalt sin against thine own people: which

requires the addition of one Hebrew letter as is done by LXX
and Syriac. RSV makes THY PEOPLE refer to Egyptians,
but either (*a*) or (*b*) makes THY PEOPLE the Israelites themselves. This piece of flattery has no effect on Pharaoh, though
it may have led to the alteration of the Hebrew text!

18. Go now, and work   The word for WORK is the same as
the word for SERVE in 4.23; 8.1, 20 (Hebrew 7.26; 8.16), etc.
Pharaoh thus refuses the request of Moses with Moses' own
word.

The quarrel between the foremen and the brothers in vv.
20f. is a natural and common occurrence amongst conspira-
tors confronted with an apparently invincible power. TURNED
AGAIN in v. 22 simply means not a journey but probably
repeated and insistent intercession, in which Moses doubts
his mission, but from which he gains the conviction that in
due course Pharaoh will be unable to maintain his absolute
refusal, and will in fact find himself in such a position that
he will be irresistibly compelled to drive out the Israelites.
Such a 'reversal' and 'recognition' afford a further illustration
of that principle of Aristotle applied by Driver to the Joseph
story in his commentary on Gen. 37-50 (pp. 319ff.).

6.1. strong hand   References to the hand are frequent in the
book, whether the hand is that of God, of Moses, of Aaron, or
of Pharaoh.

ANOTHER ACCOUNT OF THE CALL OF MOSES

6.2-7.7 P

This section describes a call given to Moses, who according to ch. 5 is in the land of Egypt. In the dispute between the brothers and the foremen (5.21), and in the uncertainty now expressed by Moses (5.22f.), a fresh call by way of confirmation and reassurance is most apposite. That Moses would go through alternating experiences of certainty and dismay is part of the life of any leader. No doubt this is what was intended by the final editor when he placed this new account of Moses' call in this particular place. Similarities abound between the account of the call of Moses in Midian related in ch. 3 and this account of the call to him in Egypt, but there are also differences in words, thoughts and outlook which show that, all things considered, this section is a different account, a Priestly account, of the same events narrated in ch. 3 (JE). This section then is not a sequel but a parallel to ch. 3, even if the writer used it at this point to show how Moses' call was re-confirmed in a difficult situation. Compare the following pairs of passages: 3.6-8, 14-15 with 6.2-8; 4.10 with 6.12b; 4.16 with 7.1; 3.19f. with 6.7 and 7.4f.

A REVELATION TO MOSES

6.2-13

The literary form is remarkable. The divine speech, 6.2-8, begins and ends with the words, I AM THE LORD. Just as a national anthem is played on the radio or television before and after the speech or appearance of a sovereign personage, so these four words isolate and authenticate the utterance of which they are part. The divine 'I' is sustained throughout

the whole passage and illustrates Israel's art of theocentric
utterance. The passage is a form of preaching in which the
preacher is God, although the passage is also a dictated ser-
mon which the Lord pronounces but Moses speaks to the
people (cp. v. 9). In fact v. 2 says God is the speaker, but v. 9
says it is Moses. The passage is an illustration of Priestly
preaching uttered by Moses but also put into the mouth of
God. The power and majesty of the passage are evident, as
well as its literary perfection.

The four words, I AM THE LORD, are one of the most remarkable sentences in scripture. They virtually say, 'The LORD is
the LORD', and as such are an example of the I-AM-WHO-I-
AM type of sentence. In these four words, so very frequent
also in Leviticus and Ezekiel, the Lord introduces himself
and proclaims himself. In this purest form of revelation, the
Lord makes himself known. These words are as W. Vischer
has said 'autokerygmatic' (self-declaratory), where the 'auto'
means God. God speaks of himself in terms of himself and
not merely in terms of one or other of his attributes. Thus,
'I am the way, the truth, the life', etc., are also autokerygmatic,
but such sentences are partial and not so complete or so
ultimate as I AM THE LORD. The only really comparable
sentences are 'I am God', 'I am He', but since LORD (in
capitals) in the EVV shows that the Hebrew has the divine
name Yahweh (Jehovah), the sentence has also a personal
quality to it not even present in the 'I am God', which expresses pure majesty. I AM THE LORD is the sovereign sentence
of all scripture, as it is also the most divinely personal and
sublime.

This passage is developed not only in its literary form but
also in its theological content. The elements are: the recollection of the revelation to the patriarchs, and the covenant with
them concerning the land (vv. 3f.); the contemporary recognition of Israel's misery in bondage, and the acknowledgment
of God's obligation to them in that condition (v. 5); the pro-

mise of deliverance from Egypt (v. 6); the promise of a
covenant (distinct from that with the fathers) (v. 7); the
promise of the possession of the promised land (v. 8). Note
how the authenticating words I AM THE LORD are repeated at
the beginning of v. 6, to introduce the predictive portion of
the oracle, the special promise of the new divine activity on
Israel's behalf. The name of God is thus closely linked with
the new revelation and with events about to happen.

The passage is more developed in its theological ideas than
ch. 3, though many of the ingredients are the same, e.g. revelation of the name; reference to the patriarchs; Israel's bondage;
the promised land, etc.

3. but by my name the LORD I did not make myself known
to them

In spite of attempts to translate these words in some other
way, or to fasten upon them some other meaning, the plain
sense is best. The Lord says in effect: 'I am the same God as
the fathers worshipped and who now makes himself known
to you. But whereas the fathers knew me as God almighty,
and did not know that my real name was YHWH, I am now
telling you that my name really is YHWH.' In effect then the
name is now made known for the first time, and so ought
never to have appeared in scripture before this point. In fact
the name does appear, and therefore must appear in passages
for which the writer of the present passage was not responsible.
Ex. 6.2 remains a key passage for the separation of at least
two kinds of material in Genesis and Exodus up to this point.
Both chs. 3 and 6 show the divine name revealed to Moses.

God Almighty Lit. *El Shaddai*; cp. other similar expressions
in the OT, e.g. *El Elyon* (Gen. 14), *El Roi* (Gen. 16), *El Bethel*
(Gen. 28), etc. The patriarchs knew God as the particular God
(*El*) who was distinguished by the epithet *Shaddai*. The Latin,
following Greek, has *omnipotent*, hence EVV ALMIGHTY. *El*

Shaddai, or simply *Shaddai*, is a very old title for God, but is not said to be associated with any cult place, and the meaning of the word is uncertain, though 'destroyer' and 'mountain' are two of the suggestions which have been made. *El Shaddai* is controlled in the Hebrew by a construction which means 'in my capacity as *El Shaddai*'.

4. I also established This is the Priestly term for covenant-making, whereas the verb in the other sources is not 'establish' but 'cut', a quite different Hebrew root and idea. MY COVENANT: this term is absent from ch. 3, though the continuity between the patriarchs and Israel in Egypt is maintained in 3.6 and 6.3f. The use of the term COVENANT in ch. 6 makes the continuity more effective and operative.

6. I will redeem This Hebrew term is used to denote a person's next of kin upon whom certain duties are laid. The Lord is Israel's kinsman, and he must as part of his duty to them rescue his distressed people.

7. I will take you for my people This is clearly a reference to the covenant which will be presently concluded with Israel after its deliverance. Although P has no account of the making of that covenant, 6.7 is clearly his anticipatory reference to it.

I WILL BE: better, 'I will become'. WHICH I SWORE—the covenant often has the form of an oath.

10-13. Moses' objection is simply overruled. His lack of eloquence is ignored and the commission reiterated.

THE FAMILY TREE OF LEVI

6.14-27

6.2-13 contain the first reference to Moses which the Priestly

writer makes, and that writer now includes a family tree of
Moses to show the context of his descent. In 1.2, Jacob's
sons were mentioned. The first three of these were Reuben,
Simeon and Levi—Jacob's three eldest sons by his first wife,
Leah. Levi's sons are Gershon, Kohath and Merari, ancestors
of those priestly families who were the servants of the later
sanctuaries. In turn Levi's grandsons are also mentioned, but
attention is directed by the mention of ages to a particular
line of descent through Kohath. Levi lived to be 137 years,
Kohath 133 years. Kohath's first-born is Amram who married
Jochebed, and these are the parents of Aaron and Moses, and
Amram lived 137 years. Details are fullest about this couple
and show both the interest and purpose of the writer. The
families of Kohath's second and fourth sons are also mentioned, but not the family of the third. Aaron's marriage and
his four sons are mentioned. Since the two oldest of these,
Nadab and Abihu, were slain (Lev. 10.1-3), the writer, after
mentioning the sons of Korah, grandson of Kohath, ancestors
of other temple servants, mentions the marriage of Aaron's
third son, Eleazar, and with the birth of Phinehas, Eleazar's
son, the family tree ends. The real line is therefore Levi,
Kohath, Amram, (Moses and) Aaron, Eleazar, Phinehas.
Moses' marriage is not mentioned, but his place in the line of
descent is clear. As elsewhere Moses and his cousins are
always in the fourth generation from Jacob's sons. Vv. 26-27
link the family tree and Moses and Aaron to the deliverance
from Egypt.

THE STORY PROCEEDS

6.28-7.7

Verses 28-30 resume the story, for v. 29 summarizes God's
words in vv. 2 and 11, and 30 repeats Moses' objection from

v. 12. So 7.1-5 goes on from 6.12, and Moses' objection is dealt with as it was in 4.15-16. On the analogy of the God-prophet arrangement, Moses and Aaron are to co-operate. They will address themselves to Pharaoh, but it will be in vain, for God (as in 4.21) will harden Pharaoh's heart, and then subsequently God will effect Israel's deliverance from Egypt. Moses at 80 and Aaron at 83 play the parts appointed for them.

THE STORIES OF THE PLAGUES

7.8-10.29

The second account of the call of Moses in 6.1-7.7 is the first additional section, as the story of the plagues in 7.8-10.29 is the second which separates the Jewellery and First-born themes as they occur in chs. 3f. and again in 11. The stories of the plagues are part of the tradition, but they are a separate part inserted at this point where the main theme of the narrative is being interrupted. In the complex of traditions ch. 11 originally and probably followed chs. 3-5, and was itself followed by the primary Passover stories to which the plague stories now serve as preliminaries.

A Separate Whole

The stories of the plagues in these chapters are a distinctive whole, a separate entity. The same characters appear throughout. In the background are the Israelites, for whom the struggle is waged, and the Egyptians who suffer willy nilly because of and with their ruler. In the foreground are Moses with his helper, Aaron, and Pharaoh with his servants, the wise men and the magicians. The controlling character on both sides is of course the Lord, the God of Israel.

The same themes appear throughout, e.g., the request for Israel's deliverance, the afflictions of the Egyptians and the obduracy of Pharaoh. Especially interesting is the role of Pharaoh in the face of such disasters. Pharaoh is seen putting forth a series of compromises in the hope of gaining his own way, but the reader of the stories knows what Pharaoh does not know, that his compromises are in vain, that his conduct has been predetermined, and that the plague stories are meant to end as they begin, with a complete deadlock between Moses and Pharaoh, and indeed a decree by Pharaoh that they are never to meet again (10.28f.). Similarly the stories show a development in the attitude of Pharaoh's magicians.

The same media appear throughout: Moses' crook, or his hand; Aaron's rod or his hand; Pharaoh's stubbornness, which is as much part of the divine will as the media on Israel's side.

Literary Diversity

Nevertheless within the uniformity of these stories there is clearly great diversity as well as some development. S. R. Driver in his commentary lists six recurring points of difference in the description of the plagues which point to the three accounts of the plagues set forth by J and E and P. Recurring differences in the words to describe the hardening of Pharaoh's heart, the plagues themselves, and other circumstances in the story also occur (Driver, pp. 55-58). Not one of the three sources has all the first nine plagues, for presumably the third plague, the gnats, is P's equivalent of the fourth plague, the dog-flies of J, and the fifth plague, the murrain on cattle, is J's equivalent of the sixth plague, P's story of the boils on men and beasts. According to Driver seven of the nine plagues occur in J, four in P and four in E. Some scholars, as Noth, doubt the presence of E, and think that both J and P figure together in five plagues (the first, second, seventh, eighth and ninth), J alone in the fourth and fifth, and P alone in the third and sixth. The reader is referred to the commentaries by Driver and Noth for further details.

More interesting is the development in the stories within of course the predetermined end. This end is predicted in 7.4, PHARAOH WILL NOT LISTEN TO YOU, and confirmed at the conclusion of these stories in 10.27. Nevertheless there is a development in the attitude both of the magicians and of Pharaoh. In the first two plagues, the magicians equal the achievements of Moses and Aaron, for they too turn water into blood, and bring frogs on the land. In the third plague, the gnats, the magicians fail and confess defeat—THIS IS THE FINGER OF GOD (8.19). The magicians do not attempt anything on the fourth (dog-flies), or fifth (murrain on cattle), or sixth (boils on men and cattle), but themselves suffer the boils, and thereafter disappear completely from the story (9.11).

Pharaoh's stubbornness is constant: though overwhelmed by frogs he appeals to Moses and Aaron for help and promises release, but, later, when the frogs are dead, changes his mind. In the third plague Pharaoh is simply defiant. In the fourth plague, however, he offers a concession. Israel may hold the proposed feast but within the confines of Egypt. Moses refuses, and then Pharaoh agrees to a wilderness feast but as close as possible to Egypt. When the plague ends Pharaoh withdraws his permission. In the fifth and sixth plagues Pharaoh is again simply defiant. In the seventh plague, the hail, Pharaoh is driven to confess his sins, request intercession and grant Israel's release. As the plague ends he becomes stubborn again. A new motif appears in the eighth plague. Pharaoh's own servants intercede with Pharaoh for Egypt's sake, and, as a result, Pharaoh lays down that Israel's menfolk alone may go to the feast. Moses refuses, the locusts arrive, Pharaoh confesses his sins and prays a fourth time for the removal of a plague, but without offering any concessions. When the locusts are removed, Pharaoh maintains his refusal. In the ninth plague, a darkness limited to three days, Pharaoh offers his greatest concession: all Israel may depart, but flocks and herds must remain behind as a surety for their return. Again Moses refuses, and the interview ends in deadlock. At the end of the ninth plague both parties maintain their positions, and the situation is almost as if the plagues had not occurred. Nevertheless, a certain variety and even progress, within the appointed limits, is observable in Pharaoh's attitude.

Character and Use

The stories of the plagues reveal themselves as a separate
entity marked by recurrent differences in words and thoughts.
In origin elements from J and P and possibly E are present,
but in their present form the stories project themselves as a
series of very realistic scenes all closely belonging to each
other. Their present form possibly points to their use. The
eighth plague lays down that the stories are to be told to
future generations (10.2 J). It would be difficult though not
impossible to tell, recite or teach all these stories, because the
intricate changes and variety of terms and formulae would be
difficult to remember exactly. It would be easiest simply to
read them on formal occasions to sanctuary congregations,
but the successive scenes are so vivid, the action so continuous,
the principal actions so few, the Pharaoh a blind figure of such
obvious ridicule, that one wonders whether the plague stories
as they now stand in scripture were not once dramatized and
performed at Passover time in religious gatherings. Since the
Passover lamb was chosen on the tenth day, perhaps the first
nine days of the month were given to the recital or performance of the first nine plagues. If the plague stories are representations of what they thought took place in Egypt, then
many problems of the present narrative would be solved, even
if others emerge. Read as the scripts of dramatic perform-
ances, the narrative gains new perspectives.

Purpose

Certainly, the avowed purposes of the plagues support a
temple occasion for their recital or performance. The plagues
are brought on Egypt in order that Pharaoh may realize that
the Lord is the Lord (7.17; 10.2), that he is unique, that he is
the God in Egypt (8.22), that Pharaoh may learn the power
and the name of the Lord (9.16), and that the earth is the

Lord's (9.29). All the descriptions of the purpose of the narrative belong to J, and of course are appropriate to religious
occasions.

Historical and Religious Value

To assess the historical and religious values of the plague
stories the historical facts must be distinguished from the
account of them. Two major facts may clearly be discerned
throughout these stories. The first is that at this time Egypt
was visited by a series of disasters of exceptional severity in
a brief space of time. The second fact is that the Egyptian
monarch, although stubborn and difficult, was nevertheless not
only a wily opportunist but a brave and resolute man.

Nevertheless, these facts, described in such a way as to
afford great enjoyment and delight to ancient Israelites, give
real concern to many readers today. The account shows that
God deliberately inflicted these plagues upon the Egyptians
and later killed the first-born in order to achieve Israel's
release. Many will prefer the doctrine that nature is neutral
(Matt. 5.45). The difficulties are not in the facts but in Israel's
interpretation of the facts.

The account likewise shows that Pharaoh's behaviour was
due to the Lord, who periodically and consistently hardened
Pharaoh's heart. Pharaoh appears as a kind of theological
ninepin, set up to be knocked down, and knocked down to be
set up again. Does God really show that he is God, that the
earth is his, that his power is without limit by making a fool
of the king of Egypt? The Israelites thought so, but such
views are difficult for us. On the other hand, as McNeile
points out, these stories are intended to teach the efficacy of
intercession, the almighty power of God, the hatefulness of
sin, the suffering of the innocent and God's concern for his
own people.

PRELUDE TO THE PLAGUES

7.8-13 P

In this passage P reports the first meeting of Moses and
Pharaoh (but cp. 7.6), and the first display of the divine
power before Pharaoh. In 4.1-5 (J) Moses is given the power
to turn his shepherd's crook into a snake as a sign to convince the Israelites. The story is part of Moses' third objection
to his call. In this passage Aaron, at God's command, throws
down his rod before Pharaoh and his servants, and it becomes
a serpent. The Egyptian magicians manage a similar feat, but
Aaron wins the contest, for Aaron's rod swallows up their
rods. Aaron's victory is in vain because Pharaoh's heart is
strong, and so the scene is laid for the struggle between God
and Pharaoh.

9f., 12. serpent Heb. *tannin*, any large reptile such as a young
crocodile. A different Hebrew word is used in 4.3 and 7.15.
MAGICIANS: the meaning of the Hebrew word is unknown, but
the word is only used in connection with Egypt and its magic.
WAS HARDENED: lit. was strong, i.e. unyielding. WOULD NOT
LISTEN: Pharaoh refused permission for Israel's departure.
7.13 resembles 6.1, for in both contexts the imminence of
stronger measures is obvious.

THE FIRST PLAGUE

7.14-25

Both J (vv. 14, 16, 18, 23-25, etc.) and P (vv. 19, 22, etc.) and
possibly E (parts of vv. 15, 17, 20) are represented. In spite of
Pharaoh's known refusal, Moses is to waylay Pharaoh at the
water's edge and is to demonstrate God's lordship by turning
the Nile into blood, and by fouling its waters with dead fish.

In the P version Aaron by his rod is to turn all the waters in
Egypt into blood. SAY TO AARON is the usual formula employed
by P. VESSELS OF (in v. 19) is not in the Hebrew. What is
meant is that the sap of trees and springs of water among the
rocks will be affected. In vv. 20 and 21 only the waters of the
river are affected, but in v. 21 (end) the blood appears throughout the entire land. Moses is probably the subject of LIFTED
UP in v. 20. But the magicians are also able to do the same,
and so Pharaoh goes home unmoved, while his waterless
people dig for water. Since presumably SEVEN DAYS (v. 25)
elapsed from the beginning of the plague until its end, it is not
explained how the magicians could have done their work,
when all the water they had was already blood, or why they
should have caused further suffering to their people and themselves. The Hebrew of v. 17 lends some support to Noth's
view that originally J's plague was simply the smiting of the
river in order to kill the fish and so pollute its waters, the
water-to-blood feature having been introduced from P. Israel
remains unaffected by this attack on Egypt's water supply.

THE SECOND PLAGUE

8.1-15

The opening formula is that of J. Moses is in Pharaoh's
palace to demand Israel's release and, if Pharaoh refuses, to
threaten him and his people with swarms of frogs from the
Nile. The frogs will be found everywhere including Pharaoh's
private quarters as well as the HOUSES (so RSV following
LXX; Samaritan and Mass. Heb. 'house') OF YOUR PEOPLE
(so RSV as LXX; Heb. UPON YOUR PEOPLE). The plague is not
a danger to Egypt but a vast inconvenience especially as the
frogs climb upon the persons of Pharaoh and his people. A
symbolic but dramatic representation of this would have been
the occasion of mirth. In vv. 5-7 the plague is said to arrive, in

the terms of P's formula, from all the waters of Egypt, and
not merely the Nile. The miraculous elements lie in the timing
of the plague and in the numbers of the frogs concerned.

THE MAGICIANS do the same and presumably increase the number of frogs and the general discomfort. So Pharaoh summons
the brothers and makes his first acknowledgment of the Lord.
The plague is sent and can be removed by God, and Moses is
the agent of its coming and so presumably of its removal.
Pharaoh promises Israel's release subject to the removal of
the frogs. BE PLEASED TO COMMAND ME: lit. have thou this
glory over me. Moses asks Pharaoh to fix a time for the removal of the frogs. The departure of the frogs at that hour will
prove to Pharaoh that God removed them and that God is in-
comparable. Moses does his part and the frogs die and are
gathered in stinking heaps. But Pharaoh does not keep his
word and remains stubborn (J). RESPITE: better, relief. Israel's
lot is not mentioned.

The unreality of the description appears at several points
but especially in Pharaoh's choice of the time for the removal
of the plague. Pharaoh is said to have chosen TOMORROW,
whereas a man in such difficult circumstances would more
naturally have said 'At once, at once!'

THE THIRD PLAGUE

8.16-19

The Priestly writer briefly describes the third plague not of
lice (EVV) but more probably GNATS, which settle on men and
beasts. Others suggest mosquitoes. The DUST of the ground,
that is, the loose top layer of soil, is turned into gnats, so there
must have been vast quantities. This story marks the first stage
in the defeat of the MAGICIANS. They cannot repeat the plague
—there is no dust left—they have been outmanoeuvred and

they acknowledge their defeat. THIS IS THE FINGER OF GOD:
this admission maddens Pharaoh and he remains hardened (P).
Israel's fate is not mentioned.

THE FOURTH PLAGUE

8.20-32

J now tells at some length the plague of flies, dog-flies or insects, and this is probably J's equivalent of the previous plague.
At the water's edge Moses is to reinforce the usual demand
for Israel's release, and the usual threat of further trouble,
with the new point that Israel will not be affected, and so
Pharaoh is warned in advance of Israel's safety in order that
when it comes about, Pharaoh will again recognize that God
is Lord. GOSHEN: the place of Israel's sojourn in Egypt, and
in the eastern delta of the Nile (Gen. 47.6,11). Probably
Goshen is the modern Wâdî Tumilât between Port Said and
Suez. It was near the Egyptian court (Gen. 45.10) and a pleas-
ant region suitable for flocks and herds (Gen. 47. 1,4,6).

23. put a division   So LXX and Vulgate: Heb. 'set redemption,' but the alteration of one letter would give the Greek
and Latin reading: P-L-T-H for P-D-T-H. The fact of the
division of the land will thus be an *'oth*, a sign, of the reality of
the power of God. GREAT SWARMS (v. 24)—EVV 'grievous'—
many and burdensome. RUINED, by suffering and disruption.

In desperation Pharaoh summons the brothers and grants
Israel a holiday to hold the sacrificial feast but within the confines of Egypt. Moses refuses the concession on the ground
that Israelite sacrifice would cause offence to the Egyptians.
The exact nature of the offence is uncertain, but presumably
Israel would sacrifice what the Egyptians would not sacrifice,
and this would annoy the Egyptians. Pharaoh accepts the
force of this and now agrees to Israel's release provided that

they do not go very far into the wilderness. Moses accepts this, promises the removal of the plague for the following day but warns Pharaoh against double-dealing. Nevertheless Pharaoh plays false, and once more a stalemate is reached.

THE FIFTH PLAGUE

9.1-7 J

After the complete breakdown of negotiations over the fourth plague, there is no possibility of discussions for the time being. So the next plague is merely carried out in the usual terms. Moses maintains his position exactly, and Pharaoh too maintains his position but investigates the fate of Israel's cattle and finds that they are safe. In spite of this Pharaoh remains stubborn and the deadlock continues.

3. plague upon your cattle A murrain—or even anthrax from the frogs. Some commentators emphasize that only the cattle IN THE FIELDS were concerned. Other cattle indoors including Israel's might then have escaped, but ALL THE CATTLE OF THE EGYPTIANS DIED (v. 6), but in spite of this see 9.9f., 19f.

THE SIXTH PLAGUE

9.8-12 P

P tells the story of the plague of boils on men and beasts, possibly an anthrax of the skin caused by the carrier fly of the fourth plague. In the deadlock Moses puts some extra pressure on Pharaoh. He himself takes kiln ashes and throws them towards heaven in Pharaoh's sight. The intention is clear. Since Moses does it, there is obviously something severe coming. But it is coming from heaven in which direction Moses

throws the ashes, and Pharaoh is powerless. Even the MAGIC-
IANS break their ranks. In face of all this Pharaoh is not merely
stubborn, or strong, but the Lord hardens, strengthens his
heart: THE LORD HARDENED THE HEART OF PHARAOH. This P
story marks an important point in the plague narratives which
Driver has noted. This is the first time in the stories that the
Lord is said to harden Pharaoh's heart. The references to this
action are as follows:

J. 10.1
E. 4.21; 10.20, 27.
P. 7.3; 9.12; 11.10; 14.4, 8; cp. 14.17.

In 4.21 (E) I WILL HARDEN and 7.3 (P) I WILL HARDEN—by
different Hebrew verbs—the action is predicted by way of
general introduction to the character and role of Pharaoh.
But for the first five plagues it does not happen. Pharaoh is
said to be merely stubborn or hard-hearted. Presumably as the
terror increases, the Lord now hardens Pharaoh's heart. All
three sources agree that the action of the Lord comes late in
the story. J puts it before the eighth plague (10.1); E during the
ninth plague (10.20); P here after the sixth. The Lord hardens
Pharaoh's heart in order to enable him to last out so that,
eventually, the final disasters may take place. In other words,
all that this apparently difficult and theologically objection-
able sentence means is this—at some time after the sixth
plague Pharaoh in sheer exasperation becomes doubly stubborn. That point of his noticeably increased obstinacy is
described in Israel's customary theocentric terms: God did it.

THE SEVENTH PLAGUE

9.13-35

This is mainly a J story with extracts from E or P in vv. 22f.,
31f., 35. Following the breakdown in negotiations and trust

after the fourth plague, a complete deadlock has persisted
through the fifth and sixth, aided by the Lord's intervention
after the sixth. The beginning of the seventh plague is marked
by the usual demand for release supported now by increasing
threats. Moses is to point out to Pharaoh that he is only alive
because of God's purpose, that the divine name and power
may be manifested. In the words YOU ARE STILL EXALTING
YOURSELF, Pharaoh is further warned against his arrogance,
but, as we have seen, it is the Lord who has hardened
Pharaoh's heart. A very severe and unparalleled HAIL is promised for the following day, but the timely warning (v. 19) will
enable those Egyptians who are heedful to take precautions
and bring their cattle indoors. Moses' timely warning is an
indication of the severity of the disaster. HIS ROD—Moses
stretches out his own rod, i.e. his shepherd's crook. This is
reminiscent of E in ch. 4. The hail, accompanied by THUNDER
(lit. voices) and continuous lightning within the hail, causes
widespread destruction in Egypt, but not in Goshen.

The build-up in dramatic features which has been taking
place since the fourth plague achieves a further step in the
sequel. For the third time Pharaoh breaks down, for the first
time confesses his sins and those of his people, acknowledges
the righteousness of God and capitulates: I WILL LET YOU GO.
This time there is no waiting for tomorrow, for Moses promises that immediately he goes out, he will spread forth his
hands, i.e., will pray for the end of the plague. This time the
end of the disaster teaches the lesson that the earth is the
Lord's. Moses however expresses his belief that Pharaoh will
not change, and will not be afraid of God. Vv. 31f. are an
additional note which throws light on the extent and the time
of the plague. FLAX and BARLEY, which ripen in January, were
smitten; but WHEAT and SPELT which came a month or so after
barley were not smitten. SPELT is a cereal inferior to wheat, but
used for bread. With the end of the plague, Pharaoh's resolution is maintained.

THE EIGHTH PLAGUE

10.1-20

This again is mainly a J story with extracts from E or P in vv. 12-13a, 14a, 15b, 20.

The account of the eighth plague specially illustrates how the variety and accentuation of the dramatic action must take precedence over the recurrent formulae of J, E and P, even though such action is contained within the static result of the entire series, namely, that Pharaoh remains obstinate.

The introductory account is much longer than hitherto. I HAVE HARDENED: this is the first and only time J mentions that God is the author of Pharaoh's hard (lit. made heavy) heart. This has been done to prolong Pharaoh's resistance, so that more and more SIGNS of ever greater potency may be shown. The whole series is so remarkable that they will be told to succeeding generations in proof that God is Lord. MADE SPORT (RV marg. mocked) is correct, for the Hebrew word means 'to divert oneself at another's expense' (Driver). This candid verb reveals the character of the plot of the stories.

3. How long will you refuse   The brothers preface a challenge to Pharaoh to humble himself before they make the usual request for Israel's release. The threat of the plague is announced, and the usual warning is expanded. TOMORROW will see a plague of LOCUSTS in numbers never before seen, which will devour everything left by the hail. The attack on the food supply is complete and Egypt faces famine. The threat of such an unprecedented disaster brings about a new feature. Pharaoh's own ministers intervene and demand that Moses should be dealt with and that Israel's menfolk may be allowed to go. Moses and Aaron are sent for and they make it plain that they must hold a pilgrimage FEAST. A special Hebrew work is used here, *hag*. The meaning of this word is not certain, but it is used to describe a festival regularly held at a fixed time and place involving a journey and sacrificial rites. Pharaoh therefore tries to drive a bargain. V. 10 must be ironical, and the real concession made plain in v. 11. Israel's men but no others may go. But the concession is an ultimatum under the terms of which they are expelled from the royal presence. Pharaoh seeks to keep back the families and cattle of the Israelites as a pledge of the return of the menfolk. This is of course quite unacceptable.

A south-east wind then brings the locusts as predicted in enormous quantities, covering the ground, causing darkness and devouring everything. The destruction is so terrible that Pharaoh hastily summons the brothers, once more confesses his sin, pleads for forgiveness and intercession. Pharaoh summons the brothers IN HASTE, and likewise Moses procures the immediate cessation of the locusts. With the close of the plague, the story ends in the usual way. In all these ways then the drama of the stories has been heightened, and the same inconclusive result, in contrast to all these dramatic elaborations, only further accentuates the tension and impending climax. No mention of Israel's separation is made.

THE NINTH PLAGUE

10.21-29

The story is mainly J (24-26, 28f.) and either E or P (21-23, 25). Without any preliminaries Moses by his outstretched hand brings a great darkness for three days on Egypt. This darkness is complete, dreadful, even tangible, but Israel is at home in light. Pharaoh summons Moses and offers his greatest concession. All Israel but no flocks or herds may go. Moses is adamant, but Pharaoh is defiant, and bids Moses depart for

ever from his presence on pain of death. Presumably the
plague ends naturally. In spite of the assertion by both Moses
and Pharaoh that they will never see each other again, they in
fact do meet (cp. 11.8; 12.31).

26. we do not know Moses insists that all the animals must
be taken, because they will not know what animals they must
offer until they reach their destination. 25 Moses makes clear
that Pharaoh himself must make a present of some sacrificial
animals, according to royal custom and slave law.

NOTE: *The Feast in the Wilderness*

Although the deliverance from Egypt is sometimes stated
in quite general terms, e.g., 3.8—I have come down to deliver
them out of the hand of the Egyptians, and to bring them up
—and cp. 3.17; 4.23; 5.2; 6.26f.; 7.2-5, 14; 9.17, 28, 35; 10.20;
11.8, 10 (J, E and P), the demand for release is often speci-
fically couched in the form of a request that the Israelites may
be allowed to hold a feast in the wilderness; 'let us go a three
days' journey into the wilderness, that we may sacrifice to the
LORD our God'—3.18; 5.1, 3, 17; 7.16; 8.27f. (J and E). The
Hebrew text of 8.26 (i.e. Hebrew 8.23) by the order of its words
lays special emphasis on the journey of three days. The request for release occurs more simply, 'let my people go that
they may serve me'—8.1, 20, 29; 9.1, 13; 10.3, 7; or in other
forms 3.12; 4.23; 5.8; 8.8; 10.9, 24, 26 (mainly J).

These references show that the feast in the wilderness has a
prominent place in the story of the Exodus according to E and
specially J, though it does not figure in P. The Hebrew word
used is in 10.9 *hag* (cp. 5.1; 13.6), well known to us from the
Arabic *hajj*—the regular feast at a shrine involving a pilgrimage and sacrifice. Three further features are also mentioned.
It is a feast to the Lord, e.g. 3.18; 5.3; the feast is obligatory—
'we must go', 8.27; 10.9 J; if the Israelites do not hold the

feast, their God will punish them with pestilence or the sword, 5.3 J.

The narrative makes clear that the feast had to be held, so that the demand to hold a feast was not a pretext to ensure departure. The feast was obligatory, but the narratives do not make clear if the feast proposed was the one said to be eventually held (ch. 24), or what the relation of the proposed feast in the wilderness was to the feast actually held in Egypt —the Passover (chs. 12-13). Pedersen for example has pointed out in his study of the Passover Legend that whereas attention up to ch. 11 is concentrated on the feast in the wilderness, we are suddenly confronted in chs. 12-13 with a feast in Egypt narrated in what are for Pedersen the categories of later Judaism. Is some explanation possible for all these features in the narrative?

If the proposed feast in the wilderness was obligatory, then presumably the time of that feast was also obligatory. The commentators have overlooked the importance of this point. To keep a feast in the wilderness meant to keep it at the right time. To keep Christmas means for us to keep it on 25 December. If this is the meaning, then the recurrent demand in the stories to hold the feast became in effect a race against time. Moses was trying to get the Israelites out in time to keep the feast at the usual time. In turn this race against time helps us to understand why the plague stories mount to a climax; why after the sixth plague the Lord hardens Pharaoh's heart, i.e. Pharaoh became doubly obstinate; and why at the end both Pharaoh and Moses lose their tempers. The time limit had run out.

The commentators are at pains to point out that at the end of the ninth plague, the position remains the same. Pharaoh is obdurate; the Israelites are not released; the mission of Moses has so far failed. All this, however, will be reversed after one further plague. It is possible, however, that Moses really had failed; i.e. he has failed to achieve the release of the Israelites in time for them to hold the feast in the wilderness at the appointed time. May we not therefore suppose that Moses decided to hold the feast at the appointed time, but not in the expected place, i.e. the mount in the wilderness (cf. 3.12) which was now impossible, but in Egypt? Hence the feast in the land of Egypt on the night of the Passover.

The commentators have generally supposed that the feast held in Egypt was a form of some pre-Mosaic nomadic feast held in the springtime with the double purpose of warding off danger and of promoting communion with the tutelary deity. The obligatory character of the feast to be held in the wilderness, and the pre-Mosaic character of the Egyptian Passover, suggest that they may be the same feast. Moses held the proposed feast at the appointed time—the night of the spring full moon—but did not succeed in holding this in the wilderness. So he hit upon the idea of holding it in Egypt instead. This change of plan gave Moses one great advantage. The Israelites were all gathered together in their homes and were not scattered. They would all be conveniently and quickly given the time for their departure and any other necessary instructions. The feast in Egypt became the rallying point for the flight, as it was also compensation for the feast in the wilderness.

The conjecture that the demand for Israel's release to hold a feast in the wilderness was a race against time, which Moses lost, and that the feast in the wilderness was replaced by a feast in Egypt—held at the appointed time—may be supported by this further fact. All the references to the feast in the wilderness occur in the first eleven chapters. (The two references to 'go' in 11.1 could imply the feast.) In other words all the references occur before the holding of the feast on the night of the Passover. There is not one single reference to the feast in the wilderness after ch. 11. This suggests that the feast in Egypt took the place of the feast in the wilderness. After Israel's release from Egypt and arrival in the wilderness with flocks and herds, etc., i.e. when all the conditions laid down in chs. 1-11 for holding the feast in the wilderness have been met, there is no word that such a feast was held. On the other hand, sacrificial feasts are held in the wilderness when Jethro presides (18.10, 12) or when Moses superintends (24.1-11), but not by one single word is there any attempt to link either of these two occasions with the feast in the wilderness proposed in chs. 1-11. The demand to hold a feast in the wilderness was somehow met, overtaken or replaced by the feast in Egypt, and the best explanation is that the appointed time for the obligatory feast (in the wilderness) was the vernal full moon, when in fact the feast in Egypt was actually held.

On the other hand, the narratives have not mentioned the necessity of holding such a feast in the earlier years of the bondage. Perhaps the demand to hold the feast was part of Moses' mission and part of the revival of Yahwism among the Israelites in Egypt. The mission of Moses would then be linked with this feast. Moses' mission is stated in 3.12 to be expressed or symbolized in an act of worship to be carried out in the wilderness.

THE PREDICTION OF THE LAST PLAGUE

11.1-10 vv. 1-3 E, 4-8 J, (? 6-7) 9-10 P.

The narrative of this chapter belongs to the few days before the final blow against Egypt is struck. V.1 is the prediction of this last blow, and vv. 2f. resume 3.21f. and so connect the events of ch. 3 with those of the last plague. Vv. 4-8 is the prediction of the death of Egypt's first-born, which is an expanded version of the prediction of 4.21-3. Vv. 9-10 is P's summary statement in which v. 9 appears to belong to a point before the plagues. If it belongs after the nine plagues then v. 9 can only refer to more calamities still to come; v. 10 belongs after the nine plagues and is a resumptive summary.

one plague more With yet a different Hebrew word (used only here in Exodus), lit. stroke, often of leprosy (contrast other words in 9.14; 12.13), the Lord announces to Moses the imminence of the knock-out blow, which will lead to the departure and indeed expulsion of the Israelites. Pharaoh WILL DRIVE them away COMPLETELY (ch. 6.1 Heb. and 12.39 and 12.33). COMPLETELY may emphasize the act of expulsion but the Syriac text suggests a slightly different meaning 'all of you' or 'with everything you have'. In face of the impending departure the Israelite men now as well as the women (3.22) are to borrow jewellery (LXX and Samaritan add 'and raiment', as in 3.22; 12.35). Jewellery—the Hebrew word—can mean utensils, objects, as well as jewellery and ornaments, but whatever articles were borrowed were of gold and silver. V.3 records part of the testimony to Moses. He was very great in Egypt, but in Num. 12.3 he is the meekest man of his time, and in 12.7 he is a unique agent in the revelatory activities of the Lord (cf. Ex. 32.10 and Deut. 34.10-12).

4. And Moses said Vv. 1-8 are particularly troublesome, for

they do not state to whom Moses spoke, but it is implied in
vv. 7f that Moses was actually speaking to Pharaoh. But 10.28f.
says that they had met for the last time. Many commentators
therefore suggest that 11.4-8 originally followed 10.28f. This
suggestion, however, overlooks the words ABOUT MIDNIGHT.
These words can only reasonably mean the midnight of the
very day on which the words were spoken. So the last plague
took place at midnight of the day when the ninth plague ended.
But, according to 12.3, 6, several days must have elapsed before the fateful midnight. Clearly 11.4-6 at least belong a few
hours before the Passover midnight and are the prelude to
12.21-27, even if vv. 7-8 are what is left of a passage that once
stood after 10.28f.

7. growl Lit. whet his tongue. MAKES A DISTINCTION: lit.
severs.

8. COME DOWN from the palace to Moses where he was. In
12.31 Pharaoh does summon the Israelite brothers into his
presence. HOT ANGER—Moses' anger matches that of Pharaoh,
but in view of the oracle he has just received, that the departure of the people is imminent, and that he is about to triumph
over Pharaoh, the anger is strange and is not explained by its
immediate context. It would be explained if it was the counterpart and sequel of Pharaoh's anger in 10.28. But as was
suggested above in the note on the feast in the wilderness,
Moses' anger may have been the reflection of his chagrin that
he had failed to secure Israel's release in time for the feast
to be held in the wilderness.

THE EGYPTIAN PASSOVER AND THE EXODUS FROM EGYPT

12.1-13.16

These chapters, which relate the climax of the sojourn in Egypt, comprise P's directions for the observance of Passover (12.1-13), and of Unleavened Bread (14-20), followed by J's account of Moses' instructions to his people, how they are to behave on their last night in Egypt and perpetually thereafter (21-28). Then follow the story of the death of the Egyptian firstborn, the Israelites' preparations to depart, and the first stage of their journey (29-39 J). P adds a chronological note, and various single directions concerning the observance of Passover (40-51). In ch. 13, P's law of the sanctity of the first-born is enacted (vv. 1-2). The next two sections are J's directions concerning Unleavened Bread (3-10), and the redemption of the first-born (11-16). Then follows a note by E concerning the choice of route by the Israelites (17-20), and the chapter ends with one of the classic OT passages concerning the guidance of God in their journeys (21-22 J).

This analysis shows that there are at least two sets of instructions for the observance of the Passover, Unleavened Bread, and the treatment of the first-born. These varying instructions either overlap or supplement each other, offer differing explanations (cp. 12.34 with 12.39), and use different terms. The usual explanation is that the duplication shows the work of the two principal sources of Exodus, namely J and P. Commentators have also pointed out the marked Deuteronomic style of certain passages such as 12.25-27a; 13.3, 5, 8-9, 11, 14-16. Noth finds this style throughout ch. 13. The application of source-analysis to legal material is, however, not so straightforward as it is to the narrative portions, so that some scholars, notably J. B. Segal, have explained the different documents as each emphasizing some particular feature of the festival, and as arranged in a broad sequence which reflect the compiler's view of the development of the Passover in Israel.

The story of Israel's last day and night in Egypt is also a primary source for the Passover laws and is a magnet for the relevant lore of the feast. Nevertheless it is very difficult to separate such traditions as tell the story of the Egyptian Passover from later laws and instructions. The problem of what happened in Egypt is further complicated by the question whether it is possible to detect in the present stories pre-Mosaic elements of the Passover. Most difficult of all is to trace the elements which are unique to the Egyptian Passover, and which may represent the mind and contribution of Moses himself. Within this general problem there is also the particular problem of the relation of the events of the fourteenth night, that is the Pesah (12.11 IT IS THE LORD'S PASSOVER), and the feast of unleavened bread for seven days. In 12.1-13 there is no reference to Unleavened Bread, but in 12.14-20, the events of the first day (Pesah) and subsequent days are closely linked. Various explanations have been offered and these may be broadly summarized as follows:

1. The Pesah (Passover of the fourteenth night) is an old nomadic firstlings feast, which may be pre-Mosaic or arose first in Egypt or in the wilderness wanderings.

2. The Feast of Unleavened Bread is a feast of Canaanite origin and the use of unleavened bread marks the separation between bread from the old crops and from the new crops.

3. After Israel's settlement in Canaan the two feasts were united into one feast at an early date.

Other scholars are beginning to offer still other explanations. It is possible that the amalgamation took place, not after Israel's settlement in Canaan, but during the patriarchal period. J. B. Segal has recently denied separate origins for the two parts of the feast. He maintains that the Passover was a New Year night festival which comprised the Pesah, i.e. the ceremonies on the fourteenth night, especially the lay manipula-

tion of the blood of the sacrificial animals, together with the
antecedents on the previous days, and which continued through
the next several days, when sacrifices were held and the eating
of leaven was prohibited. The interpretation of the Passover
as a New Year festival has been maintained by a number of
scholars, whom Segal follows at this point, though they have
generally affirmed separate origins for the two parts of the
feast (cp. J. B. Segal, *The Hebrew Passover from the Earliest
Times to A.D. 70*, OUP, 1963).

P'S LAWS AND ISRAEL'S LAST NIGHT IN EGYPT

12.1-13

1. in the land of Egypt P's laws were given to Israel at Sinai
(cp. chs. 25-31, 35-40 etc.) but the present regulations were
given in Egypt, and this is mentioned; THIS MONTH or moon,
introduces what must be a new ruling for the beginning of the
year. The Israelites had two beginnings to their years. Ex.
23.16 says the harvests lead up to the end of the year, i.e. in
what corresponds to our October (34.22). Ex. 12.2 marks THIS
MONTH, i.e. the month of the Passover, called in J and E the
month of Abib (=Babylonian 'Nisan'), our March-April, the
beginning of the year. How far back each reckoning goes is
uncertain, but P takes the Spring New Year back to Israel's
last night in Egypt. The festival then is a New Year Festival.
This chronological note in v. 2 seems to be an addition separating the TELL of 3 from 1.

3. all the congregation of Israel P's characteristic phrase describes the Mosaic Israel of the wilderness as a religious and
gathered community. The phrase is frequent in P, mainly as
THE CONGREGATION and seldom outside P. The Hebrew word is
'edah, the root of which means to appoint, *'edah* and *qahal*

meaning assembly are the two important and frequent words
among some six or seven Hebrew words to describe Israel in
assembly for various purposes. *Qahal* (Deut. and later writers)
usually, and *'edah* occasionally (never in Deut.), are rendered
in LXX by *ekklesia=church*.

tenth day   On the tenth day of this month each family (or in
the case of small families, two neighbouring or closely related
ones), are to select a one-year-old male lamb or kid without
blemish, and guard it carefully until the fourteenth day. The
selection of the animal is thus the first act of the feast, but no
generally acceptable explanation of the choice of the tenth
day has ever been offered. Some have thought that the tenth
day was specially sacred as amongst Egyptians and Muslims;
or that the tenth day began, as the twenty-first day ended, the
span of twelve holy days for the feast, as in the Babylonian
New Year Festival; or that the tenth day was the first day on
which it was known whether the feast could be celebrated in
that moon or not, i.e. by the tenth day the heliacal rising of a
fixed star had or had not taken place; or that this tenth day is
a reflection of the tenth day of the seventh month, i.e. the Day
of Atonement, (cp. also Josh 4.19, and 5.10). More convincing is J. B. Segal's view that the tenth day is one unit in a
period of time in which ritual purity had to be maintained,
(cp. the dependence of the seventh day on the third day in
Num. 19.12, 19). It is also possible that on the first nine days
of the month they recited or performed the stories of the first
nine plagues, and then on the tenth proceeded to the first
ceremony of the feast, and then, after a waiting period for
purification, to the sacrifice itself.

4. number of persons   Obviously the families were counted.
This would ensure that enough meat was provided, and also
that all were present, not only for the feast but also for the
flight. This numbering may have been the origin of the later
annual census of Israel. WHAT EACH CAN EAT: these words

EXODUS 12.4-9   111

give the index of measurement for the size of the lamb, and
help to make clear the homely character of the arrangements.

6. in the evening Lit. between the two evenings, of the fourteenth day. 'Between the two evenings' has been taken to
mean between sunset and the sight of the first star; between
the beginning of the decline of the sun and sunset; from the
time when the heat of the day began to decline until sunset.
In 30.8 the phrase describes a time when the sanctuary lamps
were lit. Whatever the phrase means, the head of each household is to select, keep and then kill the lamb. He is also to
smear some of the blood on the two doorposts and lintel of
his house. This lay manipulation of some of the blood must be
a very ancient feature of the rite, for the priestly manipulation
of blood was the priestly prerogative *par excellence* in later
Israel.

8. they shall eat The feast is nocturnal. When lambs are offered as congregational offerings, and not for individual Israelites,
they are male and are burnt. Passover is unique in that it per-
mits those who make the offering to consume the offering.

unleavened bread Heb. *mazzoth*—the word is plural and
means small pieces of bread or cakes cooked without leaven.
To bake without leaven means a speedy baking necessary on
the last night in Egypt and before the hurried departure.
Leaven also meant fermentation and so decay.

Bitter herbs May be bitter lettuce or chicory: used as a
condiment or medicinally, or later, as a memorial of the
bitterness of the Egyptian bondage.

9. not . . . raw or boiled It had to be sufficiently cooked
to prevent the eating of any blood. It was to be roasted whole,
apparently on a spit, so that the fat would drip down on to the

fire and so be burnt. This would not happen if the animal was
only boiled. Any remains were to be burnt. All these regulations seek to maintain ritual purity.

11. In this manner The Israelites are to eat the meal, with
long robes secured around the waist, wearing sandals, and
with a staff in hand, ready for the road. IN HASTE: lit. a haste
with a touch of alarm or even panic about it. The historical
basis of this is obvious, even if later the haste symbolized a
speedy transition from city to desert or from one year to the
next, as has been suggested.

It is the LORD'S passover Heb. is emphatic. It is a Passover to or for or belonging to the 'LORD'. Heb. *pesah*. The
meaning of the word is uncertain—(*a*) 'protect', 'save', (cp.
Isa. 31.5); (*b*) be lame, limp, i.e. a limping dance: (*c*)
Akkadian *paššahu*—placate; (d) 'it is the blow of the LORD'
based on an Egyptian derivative; (*e*) Arabic 'to separate'; all
have been suggested. The context suggests that the meaning
of the word is 'pass', 'pass over' and, by intention, 'share',
though in later times the Passover may mark the passing over
into the New Year.

12. I will smite Here is the bald statement of the climactic
action of the fourteenth night, and the theological crux of the
Book of Exodus. On the one hand it is the death of the first-
born and the firstlings which is the direct cause of the release
of the Israelites from Egypt. In 4.23 Pharaoh's first-born alone
is threatened, but here all the first-born are threatened. Undoubtedly the historical fact behind the story is the death of
Pharaoh's first-born and others on that particular night. Perhaps the elder sons of Rameses II, the elder brothers of
Merneptah, died before their father—as A. H. Gardiner has
suggested in his recent book, *Egypt of the Pharaohs*
(Clarendon Press, 1961). But the record is that the eldest son

in every Egyptian family, and the firstling of every beast in
Egypt was killed by God that night. No epidemic, or accident,
could have been so selective. But this is what the Israelites
believed did happen in Egypt that night. An overwhelming
disaster, such as the death of the heir apparent, must have
taken place. I AM THE LORD points as usual to the solemnity,
majesty and authority of the utterance.

THE BLOOD on the Israelite HOUSES—the word is also used
of tents—guarantees the safety of the Israelites, for God will
pass over those dwellings besprinkled by blood. NO PLAGUE:
the actual method of killing is by a plague (ch. 11.1). But how
could a plague be so selective as only to slay the first-born of
men and beasts?

MAZZOTH: THE FEAST OF UNLEAVENED BREAD

12.14-20

These verses record the instructions for ritual behaviour on
the seven days following the Passover night.

THIS DAY could refer to the first day (12.2), the tenth day
(12.3), or fourteenth day (12.6) of the month, i.e. it could refer
to the Passover events of the fourteenth day, but it could
refer to the fifteenth day, i.e. the first of the seven days of
unleavened bread which are the subject of this passage. But
since a day was counted from evening to evening, Passover
night is the first half of the first day of Unleavened Bread.
THIS DAY then embraces both feasts. MEMORIAL DAY: i.e. of
the flight from Egypt. 'YE SHALL KEEP IT'—'FEAST'—'YOU
SHALL OBSERVE' are all represented by the same Heb. root,
namely *hg*—to keep a pilgrimage feast, i.e. a pilgrimage to a
sanctuary belonged essentially to this feast, as 23.15, 17 show.
ORDINANCE: law, statute, something prescribed. God makes
the ordinance or statute, and thereby imparts grace. God's

word, whatever form it takes, always originates from, and
conveys, grace.

15. first day Leaven is prohibited for seven days, and
THE FIRST of these, on the evening-to-evening reckoning, must
be from 14 to 15, so as to permit of seven days by the twenty-
first day of the month (so 12.18 precisely). The first and
seventh days are also to be marked by assembly. Obviously
this must be part of later regulations, for the 14/15 day of
the Egyptian Passover was spent in flight. The first and last
days could be used for the preparing of food so they were not
so holy as Sabbath or Day of Atonement.

17. I brought The verb is past tense, though the actual
departure is still before us—obviously a rubric belonging to
later time, or this passage should be removed to after v. 36.

ANOTHER ACCOUNT OF THE PASSOVER

12.21-28

This account, which may come from the J source, confirms
the lay selection of the lamb, and its slaughter, and the
manipulation of the blood. It confirms too the Lord's Passover and sparing of Israel, but introduces several new features.
The ELDERS are the recipients of the instructions, and they are
to use a bunch of HYSSOP dipped into the blood to smear the
houses with the blood. The function of the hyssop was to
draw off any dangerous power in the blood—it acted as a
'lightning conductor' (Segal). HYSSOP is probably one of the
species of marjoram. BASIN could be translated threshold, but
a container of some sort is surely intended. The Israelites are
to remain indoors all night, and thus they will be preserved.

23. the LORD will pass over the door This is a curious way

of saying 'pass over or by the house'. Trumbull possibly interprets the words correctly by supposing that the words mean:
The Lord will pass over the door-opening, i.e. into the house,
and then from within the house prevent the DESTROYER from
entering TO SLAY YOU. Here again is a suggestion that the
slaughter was not done by the Lord but by a destroying agent
(12.23), cp. 12.13: 'no plague shall fall upon you to destroy
you'. If Trumbull has the correct interpretation, then the
blood is not apotropaic, i.e. to ward off evil; but it identifies
for God the houses of the people where he enters for the
covenant meal of the Passover. The feast is then, as it eventually became, a festival to celebrate a visiting and redeeming
God.

The annual recital of the story will instruct successive
generations of young people in the heroic events of the
ancestral flight from Egypt. The worship of the people was by
means of prostration, and again the verse mirrors later
observance. V. 28 records the carrying out of the instructions
given by Moses and Aaron in vv. 1-13. Perhaps v. 28 once
followed v. 13.

THE DEATH OF THE FIRST-BORN AND THE DEPARTURE OF THE ISRAELITES

12.29-39 J, 40-42 P

This section resumes 11.4-6 and reports the death of the first-
born of men and cattle by sudden, selective supernatural
action. The record demands more than the death of the royal
heir (4.23), and suggests some epidemic, like poliomyelitis because mainly young people were affected. But polio does not
affect cattle. Difficulties attend every explanation except the
fact of the magnitude of the disaster, which caused Pharaoh
to rise IN THE NIGHT and in spite of his former protestation

never to see Moses again (10.28), to summon MOSES AND
AARON. By obeying this command, the brothers infringe the
command of 12.22, that nobody must go outside. The story,
however, requires this, for they receive the command to
depart. AS YOU HAVE SAID can only refer to the feast in the
wilderness under all the conditions the brothers had laid down
to Pharaoh. BLESS ME ALSO: the king even hopes to share in
the festival blessing, and this request suggests that he expects
to see them back in Egypt. The Israelites thus depart, indeed
they are requested to go. In readiness for the flight they had
borrowed jewellery and finery from the Egyptians. Since they
were really not intending to return, the borrowing was really
robbery. They had also packed. Apparently they had unleavened DOUGH with them but they had not prepared any
food (v. 39), so, later, on the flight, they quickly baked
unleavened cakes with this dough they had brought from
Egypt.

37. Raamses to Succoth   For RAAMSES see 1.11 SUCCOTH is
Hebrew for *tkw*, probably Tell El-Maskhuta, near Pithom, in
the eastern Wâdī Tumilât, between Suez and the Mediterranean. This is a short stage for the first journey, far enough to
be some distance away, but not too long following a night
vigil.

six hundred thousand men . . . besides women and children
There must have been a quick check to find out if all the
families had got away and also 1.11 shows that the Israelites
were in two centres at least. The first company must have
'called for' a second company, or made a rendezvous, and
this would involve further counting. The figure 600,000
men implies the same number of women, and children at
the rate of one per adult would not be excessive. So the
company envisaged here is over two millions, a figure not
compatible with Goshen, with the wilderness, with the

crossing of the sea or the journey to Canaan. To have sprinkled
blood over such a community (24.8), or to station them at the
foot of a mountain (19.2) would have been impossible tasks
in the time and areas possible. The figures are given several
times (38.26; Num. 1.46; 11.21), and must represent the
Israelite population, say, of David's day. A MIXED MULTITUDE
(v. 38), labourers other than Israelites. They form a group,
scarcely worth mentioning besides two million people, but
distinctive in size and character among the numbers of
Israelites who did depart (cp. Num. 11.4; Deut. 29.11; Josh.
8.35).

41. four hundred and thirty years   This is stated to be the
length of the sojourn in Egypt. Gen. 15.13 has four hundred
years. The reading of the Samaritan and Greek texts could
halve the period to 215 years. But Gen. 15.16 and Ex. 6.13-20
make clear, as do other passages, that the fourth generation
of Israelites from Jacob accompanied Moses out of Egypt.
Four generations would make the period of the sojourn about
one century. HOSTS suggests later military terminology.

42. night of watching   The Lord had been wakeful throughout
Passover night, and the people too had kept vigil. This is the
covenant note of Passover night, retained and observed in
perpetuity in Israel. First nights are memorable, especially
God's first nights in the soul. Paul often recalled the Damascus
road.

PERMITTED PARTAKERS OF THE FEAST

12.43-51

This supplementary group of laws prescribes the Israelite
character of Passover, by denying the right of any foreigner

to partake. Purchased slaves if circumcised may partake.

45. No sojourner or hired servant   No settler or foreign hired servant may participate.

48. a stranger   A resident alien and the males of his family, if circumcised, may keep the feast. Israel must keep it, house by house, the animal in each house to be eaten within that house. Its bones must not be broken (Num. 9.12; John 19.36). COME NEAR implies the approach to the altar, and therefore a different liturgical context from the present domestic scene. The emphasis on ALL Israel (v. 47), on the individual completeness of each household and the undivided lamb illustrate the unity.

SANCT·ITY OF THE FIRST-BORN WITH A PARENTHESIS CONCERNING UNLEAVENED BREAD

13.1-16

This section is either a miscellany (1-2, 3-6, 7-10, 11-16), or essentially a short code dealing with the first-born (1-2, 11-16) with a parenthesis concerning unleavened bread (3-10). Deuteronomistic words and ideas are present in vv. 3-16: cp. Deut. 16.1-10. RSV conceals the fact that whereas YOU in vv. 3f. is plural, YOU in vv. 5-16 is singular in Heb.

1-2. Probably P's general principle concerning the first-born of women and female beasts. Such FIRST-BORN belong to the Lord. Other law codes add other regulations concerning first-born. (See Driver, *ad loc.*) It is worth adding that a parchment fragment found in a cave near Engedi preserves parts of 13.11-16, and the fragment closely follows the Massoretic text except for one spelling difference. FIRST TO OPEN: a quasi-technical term.

3-10. THIS DAY: in v. 3 THIS DAY appears to have ended, cp. CAME OUT, but in v. 4 THIS DAY you are going forth—a participle of present or imminent action. The day is the fifteenth of Abib, the first month, the month of young ears of corn. NO LEAVENED BREAD is to be eaten that day or for seven days. The SEVENTH DAY will also be marked by a pilgrimage feast. In 12.14-20 this feast falls on the first day with holy assembly and no work on the first and seventh days. TELL is the birth of *kerygma* (LXX *anaggelleis*, cp. I Cor. 11.26) based on personal experience and testimony. AND IT SHALL BE, i.e. the keeping of this feast will be what tattoo-marks on the hands, and some ceremonial dress over the forehead and eyes will be in other connections, namely, a sign full of meaning, and a reminder full of relevance of a salvation enjoyed and a law to be obeyed. YOU SHALL . . . KEEP the feast annually at the appointed time and in the land promised to the ancestors of the Israelites.

11-16. These elaborate the principle of vv. 1-2. The law concerns male first-born of women, who must be redeemed, and male firstlings of beasts which are God's. By inference Lev. 11.1-8, and Deut. 14.3-8 suggest that the ass could not be eaten or slain as a sacrifice, so that either a lamb—of less value be it noted—had to be slain in its stead, or the ass's neck broken—i.e. it was not to be killed in a sacrificial way.

14. you shall say The confessional statement is longer and includes again history and duty. THEREFORE I SACRIFICE: i.e., all the male firstlings of beasts, but male first-born of men are redeemed. The performance of this law is also like a tattoo-sign or like FRONTLETS between the eyes. FRONTLETS, lit. droplets(?) or something worn, were originally jewellery, badges, but later phylacteries or *tephilloth*, little cases containing certain verses (Ex. 13.1-10, 11-16; Deut. 6.4-9; 11.13-21) on small pieces of scroll, attached by thongs to forehead and left arm.

The treatment of the first-born (even if the firstlings of beasts are a later expansion), the blood rites of Passover night, and the prohibition of leaven, are the three themes of Exodus complex. Each one is a story of, or is linked by a story to a major feature of the Exodus. Each one is an essential part of the *Credo* which is to be passed on to later generations (cp. Ex. 12.25-27; 13.8f., 14-15) and each one is for repetition as by law prescribed. To claim that any one or more of these themes originally had nothing to do with the Exodus is precarious. More important is to ask wherein lies Moses' own contribution to the practice and thought of the Egyptian Passover. Was it Moses, for example, who became convinced in advance that Pharaoh's first-born would die (4.23)? Was it Moses who, having failed to get Israel out in time to keep an ancient feast in the wilderness at the right time, hit on the idea of holding it in Egypt instead, but also linked that feast with his own mission of salvation and the Lord's judgement in Egypt? J. B. Segal claims a parallel between the actual Passover and the modern Arab sacrifice *fedu* or *fidyah*—a spring offering including blood smearing to redeem families at the New Year. Compare Heb. *pdh* which is used at 8.19 (Ex. 8.23): 'I will put a division', i.e. redemption. . . . In other words the influence of Moses at Passover may be seen in the interpretation of the feast away from the old apotropaic idea towards a more positive note of divine Parousia and redemption.

THE MIRACULOUS WAY TO AND
THROUGH THE SEA

13.17-14.31 J, E, P

All three sources bear testimony to Israel's miraculous guidance to, and deliverance at, the sea. P is clearly found in 14.1-4, 8, 15-18, 22-23, 26, 28-29, and parts of 9, 10, 21 and 27. J is seen in 13.20-22, 14. 5-7, 11-14, 20, 24, 25, 30-1 and parts of 9, 10, 19, 21 and 27. E appears in 13.17-19, and possibly in 14.5a, 6, 15, 16, and 19a, b.

17. God did not lead them This could be interpreted in two ways (*a*) they did not go this coastal way for, though this was the direct route, military forts in Egypt and border outposts in south-west Palestine might have involved them in fighting. Instead they took a more inland route. (*b*) They actually went by the coastal route, but soon realized that this was not the way the Lord led them, i.e. they were going the wrong way, because it led into a guarded frontier. They then, after a detour to Baal-zephon, turned inland to the proper route. WAY OF means of course 'way to', the usual military and commercial route. THE PHILISTINES were not to settle until later, but the area is described from the point of view of the later writer.

18. led . . . round Better, turned them round, caused a change in the direction of their journey. WILDERNESS TOWARD THE RED SEA: i.e. the Egyptian wilderness south of Tumilât, and west of the northern end of the Gulf of Suez, the northwest extension of the Red Sea. RED SEA: lit. Sea of Reeds, possibly Lake Timsah, or a stretch of water no longer existing between Gulf of Suez and Timsah. The Heb. name also refers to the Gulf of Suez and the Gulf of 'Akaba. The location of the crossing is therefore uncertain. This is the so-called southern route of the Exodus.

19. God will visit you I.e., they will surely depart from Egypt. Moses is said to take the bones of Joseph with him. Popular memory and feeling shine through this incident.

20-22. From Succoth to Etham, site unknown, is the first stage of the journey by the combined groups. The journey is by divine guidance—the pillar of cloud and fire reflects the wayfarers' recollection of desert experiences. Vv. 21-22 are a classic statement of the Lord's guiding Presence. See Driver *ad loc.* for his account of three descriptions of the Presence of God in Exodus.

14.1-4. TO TURN BACK : P records the decision to change route, (cp. 13.17 above). The first stage of the altered route actually takes them nearer to the Mediterranean sea. PI-HA-HIROTH is unknown, but BAAL-ZEPHON is on a hillock at the western end of the strip of land dividing the Sirbonian sea—Lake Berdawil —from the Mediterranean. Migdol is also on this route—the so-called northern route of the Exodus. Israel began to go along the northern route, then changed to the region around Baal-zephon on the coast; and after crossing the sea went south to the southern route. This round-about route after the crossing was intended to deceive any would-be pursuers.
HAS SHUT THEM IN : i.e., they are not in the wilderness, but in Egypt and hemmed in by the wilderness. I WILL HARDEN refers to the recurrence of that extra wilfulness of which Pharaoh was capable. The thoughts and expressions of v. 4 are those of the theology of P.

THE DELIVERANCE AT THE SEA

14.5-31

V. 5 does not necessarily contain two accounts of the depar-

ture of Israel. By the word FLED, a tradition of flight without
the knowledge of the Egyptians is suggested, but the rest of
the verse suggests that the Egyptians had permitted the
Israelites to depart. On the other hand, and more likely, the
word FLED points to their realization that the Israelites had
departed not merely for a pilgrimage feast, but had gone for
good. Pharaoh resolves on a personally directed pursuit.

7. with officers The meaning is uncertain—the Heb. could
be read as (*a*) a third man, but a three-man chariot is Hittite
rather than Egyptian, unless the importance of the occasion, so
far as Egypt's pride was concerned, demanded a third man;
(*b*) a man of third rank—such a contemptuous crew as these
runaways only needed soldiers of the third rank (though in
fact Pharaoh himself went); (*c*) the officers in charge were
men of rank, e.g. knights, cp. 15.4. DEFIANTLY: lit. with a high
hand, deliberately, i.e., in not proposing to return. The
Israelites, frightened by the sight of the Egyptians, reproach
Moses with a rebuke (vv. 11f.) said to have been previously
uttered in Egypt. 5.21 is the nearest approach to this rebuke.
MOSES SAID: Moses reassures his people with the thought that
if Pharaoh is leading the Egyptians, the Lord is leading
them and will bring about this deliverance. SALVATION
means a military victory as the outcome of the holy war
(battle), and Israel's escape. YOUR ROD (v. 16) suggests E, as
in 4.17.

17. and I will harden Lit. make strong—the resolve of the
Egyptians is strengthened. Despair as well as obedience to
Moses' words leads Israel towards the waters—heightened
anger leads the Egyptians to the pursuit. Increase of glory
will accrue for God in the defeat and death of Pharaoh and
his host. V. 19 describes two kinds of divine intervention. E
says that the ANGEL OF THE LORD, the invisible presence, which
had been leading the Israelites, takes up a stance between the

two companies, whereas J speaks of the PILLAR OF CLOUD in this position.

20. and the night passed   Lit. 'and it (the pillar of cloud of v. 19b) lit up the night.' The verse is difficult but possibly means no more than that the pillar of fire accentuated the surrounding darkness. As God defends them at their rear, so he also prepares the way ahead.

V. 21 says that an EAST WIND blew all night and kept the waters back. V. 16 says Moses divided the waters with his ROD, and the Israelites were able to walk on a dry sea-bed with walls of waters standing on each side of them. The passage records a supernatural interference with the waters, whether that was done immediately by the raising of Moses' arm with its rod, or more gradually and all through the night by a strong wind. The Israelites believed they had seen, and had been saved by, a great miracle which was to become one of the themes of their story and worship in perpetuity. MORNING WATCH (v. 24): from 2-6 a.m. By this time the Egyptians had gone right into the middle of the waters, but God was closely watching them, caused great panic among them, and finally clogged their CHARIOT WHEELS in the sands. LET US FLEE: the Heb. is singular, 'let me flee.' At that moment Moses' HAND—outstretched again by divine command—with the dawn brought the waters back. The entire Egyptian host was drowned and by rushing into the returning tide, was washed up dead on the shore. WONTED FLOW—perennial or usual level or flow. Pharaoh is not explicitly said to have been involved, but the last reference to him in 14.17 implies his death.

30f. EGYPTIANS DEAD: Heb. Egypt dead. GREAT WORK: Heb. great hand. Israel feared God and put their trust in, committed themselves to Moses. TO BELIEVE IN is not merely give credence to, but accept Moses as a leader. Moses is described as God's servant only three times in the Pentateuch but often in Joshua.

If some details of the events are uncertain, there is no doubt that a detachment of Egyptian soldiers, in their attempt to overtake and capture the departing Israelites, were themselves caught and destroyed in the midst of a sea. The Israelites were free to pursue their flight.

THE SONGS AT THE SEA

15.1-21

With the Egyptian threat at an end and with their own freedom now assured, the Israelites vent their relief, their triumph
and their thanksgiving in two ways; the Song of Moses and
the people (vv. 1-18), and the Song of Miriam and the women
(vv. 20-21). With one difference in the opening Heb. word:
I WILL SING (v. 21, SING), Miriam's song is identical with 15.1.
The usual view of this identity is that Miriam's song is original
in this context, and that Moses' song is an elaboration of this
early song. Miriam's song is so short that it requires the
context of the tradition or the event itself for its full understanding. It is reasonable to suppose that Miriam's song is
contemporary.

The decision concerning the Song of Moses is difficult. This
glorious song, one of the most wonderful in the entire Bible,
has the form of a hymn of praise in the first person in vv. 1-2.
The first-person form does not reappear. V. 3 crowns this
introduction, and is the text for the narrative in vv. 4-10.
Hymnic traits reappear in vv. 11-12, and then a wilderness-to-
Palestine narrative appears in vv. 13-17, followed by a hymnic
conclusion (18). This analysis shows that vv. 1-12 belong to
the tradition or event of the sea, whereas vv. 13-17, which
refer largely to the journey to and settlement in Canaan, do
not. Vv. 1-12 may then be Mosaic or have a Mosaic basis.
Perhaps vv. 1-3 is Moses' own song and Miriam used its first
verse as an antiphony to each of the verses or lines of her
brother's song.

The metre throughout is uneven. There is a marked pre-
ference for two-beat stichoi throughout. Vv. 1, 4, 6, 7, 9-13,

15a, 16a, 17, 18 comprise only two-beat stichoi, but vv. 2-3
appear to be 3-2 metre and quite distinctive in the song. No
stanza arrangement is apparent.

Whatever be the truth about vv. 1-3 or 1-12, the Palestinian
addition in vv. 13-18 has led scholars to ascribe the whole
song to dates varying from within a century of the settlement
to exilic or even post-exilic days. Nothing in the song requires
a date later than Solomon's days and if SANCTUARY in v. 17
means 'temple', it would most naturally mean Solomon's
Temple.

Accordingly, scholars have thought of the Song as a Passover Cantata, an Enthronement Hymn with or without a
connection to the renewal of the covenant, a New Year hymn
celebrating God's kingship in harvest. Most of these theories
stem from the belief that the entire song arose out of Israel's
cult, from which the J and P versions of the sea miracle were
expanded.

THE SONG OF MOSES

15.1-18

1. Moses and the people Between them they composed and
sang this song, though an individual only is concerned in
vv. 1-2. FOR: Heb. *ki*—. *Ki* is significant for the understanding
of Hebrew poetry, as it generally introduces the reason and
justification for the act of worship. I WILL SING TO THE LORD
because. . . . Similarly this whole song is grounded in its
present context by the first word of v. 19, FOR.

TRIUMPHED GLORIOUSLY: the same Heb. word is used for
both these words in a construction to emphasize the action.
The rare Heb. word means to rise loftily, the phrase seeks
to convey a sense of majesty. AND HIS RIDER: i.e., cavalry-
man—Egypt did not employ cavalry at this time—hence the

word may mean the rider in the chariot—the horse and its
chariot.

2. The LORD Heb. *Yah*—the short form of the divine name
as in Halleluj*ah*. The long form YHWH occurs at the end of
v. 3. MY SONG: Heb. a song, MY should be added as RSV does.
THE LORD is the source of the singer's strength and the object
and theme of his song (cp. Ps. 118.14; Isa. 12.2). I WILL PRAISE
HIM: this Heb. word occurs only here, and but for the paral-
lelism would be uncertain. MY FATHER'S GOD: i.e. ancestral
God. This confessional series of affirmations is crowned with
what must be, in the light of Ex. 3-6, a very Mosaic sentence:
THE LORD IS HIS NAME. Perhaps this was the climax of the
original Mosaic song.

4-10. The narrative of the Lord's victory, and the particular
example of the general principle of v. 3.
    AND HIS HOST: the same Heb. noun is used in 14.4, 9, 17,
28, of Egypt, but is not the same as that used by P in 6.26;
7.4; 12.17, 41, 51; and in Numbers of Israel. PICKED OFFICERS:
lit. the choice of his third men—see 14.7 for the same word.
FLOODS: plural of word for 'deep' in Gen. 1.2—poetic word
for deep waters.

6. Thy right hand, O LORD, glorious The comma in RSV
before GLORIOUS should be omitted because GLORIOUS (masc.)
probably belongs to LORD (masc.) and not HAND (fem.). The
removal of that comma makes this glorious verse even more
glorious! . . . . O glorious LORD.
    THY MAJESTY: same Heb. word as in v. 1, TRIUMPHED GLOR-
IOUSLY. LIKE STUBBLE—consuming like stubble is a strange
figure for death by drowning. BLAST OF THY NOSTRIL, i.e.,
anger rather than wind. The verbs are reminiscent of the P
story in 14.15ff. CONGEALED: Heb. 'solidified'.
    To the abundance of nouns in vv. 4-8, the verbs in v. 9

offer a striking contrast. The short verbal sentences describe
the confident assumptions of the enemy in his own words.
THE SPOIL: always a concomitant of victory, but here of the
recovery of their own jewellery and raiment borrowed by the
Israelites. MY DESIRE: Heb. 'my soul', as the seat of desire
according to the OT. See the references in Driver, *ad loc.*
DESTROY THEM: Heb. 'dispossess them'—the same Heb. word
in 34.24 for RSV's 'I will cast out'.

WITH THY WIND (v. 10): the Heb. word for spirit and wind is
the same. Here the wind causes the water to cover the Egyptians. In 14.21 the wind uncovers dry land, but when the wind
drops the waters return.

The sea part of the poem ends with the hymnic theme of
the incomparability of God, illustrated by the one essential
fact of the present context—the destruction of the Egyptians.
AMONG THE GODS suggests a polytheistic background. GLOR-
IOUS DEEDS. Heb 'praises', i.e., praiseworthy attributes, or
better, acts, to parallel DOING WONDERS i.e. wonders as supernatural and astonishing acts of divine origin. THE EARTH
SWALLOWED THEM: actually the sea swallowed them. It has
been suggested that Israel's way through the waters was due
to a temporary rising of the sea bed. The collapse of this portion of sea bed, as gases beneath dispersed, would accord
with the description of this verse. They went down with the
ground.

13-17. A hymnic narrative of the journey to, and settlement
in, Canaan.

13. by thy strength   The reference is almost certainly to the
ark, which is known by this description in many places in the
Psalms, cp. e.g. 78.61 (RSV 'his power') and 132.8 (RSV 'thy
might'). HOLY ABODE: lit. 'homestead of shepherds', and so
habitation in general. The reference could be to Zion or more
probably the whole land.

14ff. The peoples General references to the panic of neighbouring peoples in vv. 14 and 16 sandwich particular references to PHILISTINES (who first heard of the Exodus), to CHIEFS, or clan chiefs, of Edom, to LEADERS, mighty men (the same Heb. word as for rams) of Moab, to the inhabitants of CANAAN. This list corresponds to the route of the Exodus (Deut. 2.1-9, 18).

THOU HAST PURCHASED : the verb can mean 'create', but 'get, acquire by purchase', as a figure of redemption, is more suitable here (cp. Gen. 14.19, 22; Deut. 32.6).

MOUNTAIN . . . ABODE . . . SANCTUARY (v. 17) can all refer to Canaan in general, or Zion and its Temple in particular, or by a narrowing of definition—Canaan-Jerusalem-Temple. Albright and others deny the reference to the Temple, quoting the Ras Shamra reference to Baal's house 'on the mountain of his inheritance'. On any view the verse demands Canaanite provenance. Compared with v. 18, 17 is a long verse. Perhaps v. 18 should begin with the words THE SANCTUARY; this would then bring more closely together the idea of sanctuary and kingship which is a theme known in Near Eastern myth and ritual. WILL REIGN : the verb is future, though normally in the perfect or past tense in enthronement psalms.

THE SONG OF MIRIAM

15.19-21

V. 19 is a prose addition linking the song to 14.23, 28. V. 20 briefly introduces MIRIAM and her song. She is described as Aaron's sister. This may mean nothing more than that she is usually associated with Aaron, and sometimes with Aaron against Moses. Others have, of course, claimed that Aaron and Miriam were not related to Moses, but were once indepen-

dent figures in a larger tradition, now lost. Later they were
made members of Moses' family.

20. went out   I.e. from their dwellings, or even from the camp,
as women were wont to do, cp. Judg. 11.34; I Sam. 18.6.

PART II

ISRAEL IN THE WILDERNESS
15.22-18.27

FROM THE RED SEA TO THE MOUNTAIN OF GOD

15.22-17.16

After the victory over the Egyptians in the Sea of Reeds, the Israelites now begin their sojourn in the wilderness, of which 15.22-18.27 covers the first period. This first period includes the journey to Mount Sinai and several incidents en route. The remainder of the Book of Exodus is occupied with the second period in the wilderness, with the events which happened and the laws given at Sinai. When the visit to Sinai is completed, the third period of the sojourn in the wilderness—the so-called wilderness wanderings—begins (Num. 10.33).

FROM THE RED SEA TO ELIM

15.22-27

Attributed by different scholars to J or E. Perhaps 22b-26 are J and 22 and 27 are P.

The Israelites journey from the Sea of Reeds through the Wilderness of Shur *via* Marah to an oasis at Elim. SHUR: otherwise Etham (Num. 33.8). According to Gen. 25.18 Shur is east of Egypt, and is an eastern frontier district of Egypt; according to I Sam. 15.7 and 27.8 it is within striking distance of southern Palestine. After crossing this waterless waste they reach MARAH, where Moses finds a way of sweetening the bitter water in the well in response to the people's complaints. At 15.24 McNeile in his commentary gives a list of Israel's murmurings and rebellions on some dozen occasions. MARAH may be the modern Ain Hawarah, but the reference to statute and ordinance and the grumbling concerning water are

reminiscent of events at Kadesh (Num. 20.1-13), either Ain
Qudeis or perhaps better Ain Qudeirat.

25. HE PROVED THEM points to the Massah theme of Ex.
17.1-7 which is bound up with the Meribah theme, and the
waters of Meribah are at Kadesh (Num. 20.13). Marah then
may be at Kadesh, so that they visited Kadesh before reaching
Sinai, as they presumably stayed there for 'many days' (Deut.
1.46). The Deuteronomic IF (v. 26) carries the promise of
healing as the reward of obedience—obviously a moral added
to a story. ELIM: terebinths—oasis of unknown location. Wâdī
Gharandel, about sixty miles from Suez on the western side
of the Sinai Peninsula, is the most likely suggestion.

MANNA AND QUAILS

16.1-36

This is mainly a P story, (J in 4-5, 28-30), which must be compared with the manna and quails story in Num. 11. If the analysis is correct, then the present story is P's account of the supernatural provision of manna and quails for hungry Israelites in the wilderness. P's account is interlaced with some J or JE extracts concerning the provision of manna only. In Ex. 16 in the P portions, little is made, and in J, nothing is made of the quails. In Num. 11 on the other hand JE record that the Israelites and their fellow travellers, tiring of an exclusive manna diet, request meat, and a surfeit of quails is blown from the sea. In JE then the Israelites are given manna at the beginning of the desert period and quails later, after the visit to Sinai is over. In P, however, manna and quails are given from the beginning. The comparison of these stories has led to the generally held view that manna belonged to the original story in Ex. 16, but the quails is a post-Sinai story. Both manna and quails are natural to the conditions of the Sinai Peninsula. Manna still found under that name consists of small white drops, the secretions of certain insects. These drops are light in colour and weight, sticky and sweet, and while they harden at night, they quickly melt in the sun. They are compounded of pectin mixed with three basic kinds of sugars (see the *Interpreter's Dictionary of the Bible*, article on 'Manna'). Quails, small game birds of the partridge family, regularly appear on the western coast of the Sinai Peninsula during the northern migrations in spring and southern in autumn, when they fly in large flocks a few feet above the ground. They fly with the wind and generally alight at night to rest, when they are easily taken. It was in the supply of manna and quails in such quantities at the right place and time, and with double quantities on Fridays, that the Israelites discovered the divine provision for their needs. (Cf. F. S. Bodenheimer, 'The Manna of Sinai', *The Biblical Archaeologist* 10, Feb. 1947, pp. 2-6; now in *The Biblical Archaeologist Reader.*)

16.1-12. wilderness of Sin   Between Elim (? Gharandel) and Sinai the Israelites halt at the wilderness of Sin, lodging at the Sea of Reeds en route (so Num. 33.10f.). Assuming Sinai to be in the traditional location, towards the apex of the Sinai Peninsula, and not at Kadesh, or east of 'Akaba, then the wilderness of Sin could be Debbet er Ramleh, a broad and stony plain in western Sinai, or el Markha, a coastal plain. Neither lies on the direct route between Gharandel and Sinai, and the locations must remain indefinite (see Driver's Commentary on this passage). FIFTEENTH DAY OF THE SECOND MONTH: Noth interprets this as meaning that Israel have been six weeks on the way, but if they began their journey on the fifteenth day of the first month, then they have been a month on the way. Long halts at the places mentioned, or more stopping places, must be assumed. MURMURED: P's first mention of the people's discontent. FLESHPOTS suggests a standard of diet which slaves would hardly be likely to attain, but complaints have their natural exaggerations.

4-8. The extract from J in 4-5 promises a rain of bread from heaven and is notable also in that J also records the double quantity on Fridays. A DAY'S PORTION EVERY DAY: the thought is paralleled in the Lord's Prayer. The daily obedient collection of the manna is part of the divine testing or discipline of Israel (cp. 15.25; 17.2; Deut. 8.2; 13.3). P resumes in 6, and the people are reminded that God himself brought them from Egypt (ch. 3). The thought is dominated by the words AT EVENING and IN THE MORNING, emphatic by their position in Heb. and RSV, and as the predicted times when God would reveal his glory through the provision of food, quails at night and manna in the mornings. V. 8 crowds the passage, duplicating v. 7 and may be an editorial explanation of vv. 6-7. Perhaps vv. 9-12 should precede vv. 6-7 because Moses announces to the people in v. 6 what he is yet to hear from God in v. 12. V. 9 is interesting because AARON is the chief officiant; BEFORE THE LORD implies the Tent of Meeting—not yet of course erected. The LORD anticipates Aaron's action by appearing forthwith, promising Moses quails that night and bread next morning, and so it fell out.

The glory of the LORD Something like a brilliant and glowing appearance of fire veiled in a cloud. This is P's frequent description of the manifestation of God in connection with the Tent of Meeting. The glory is the outward and visible manifestation of the being of God, the envelope of his holy presence. AT TWILIGHT, Heb. 'between the two evenings' as 12.6. QUAILS arrive in vast quantities. In Num. 11 they cause a plague; in the present narrative nothing more is heard of them and the manna occupies the whole story. V. 12 ends with the usual authenticating formula.

13-21. *Manna. What it is and what to do with it.*

With the dispersal of the morning DEW the manna was discovered all around. The Israelites asked WHAT IS IT (*man hu*)? The words are a popular etymology and *man* may be Aramaic or Canaanite for 'what', or a corruption of an Egyptian word, but it is uncertain. THE BREAD—manna is a substitute for bread. The Israelites were to gather AN OMER (only in this chapter; about 6½ pints) per head, though, whatever a man gathered, it came always out miraculously to the right quantity of an omer per head. APIECE: lit. per head (Heb. *gulgoleth*, skull). The manna was to be eaten fresh daily. Some Israelites left some

overnight, and it went bad, and what remained on the ground
ungathered melted. Enough for each day was always given.

22-36. *Manna and Rest.*

On Fridays they discovered that the quantities gathered came
to TWO OMERS apiece, enough for Saturdays—the Sabbath—
also. The double ration of manna on Fridays—the weekend
collection—supports the principle of the sabbath rest. In
response to the report of the LEADERS—rulers—princes, lit.
those lifted up, Moses makes known the divine requirement of
the Sabbath rest.

23. A day of solemn rest   There is nothing in the Heb. or in
the word to correspond to SOLEMN. 'A day of rest' is P's
technical expression for New Year's Day, first and eighth
days of Tabernacles, Sabbath and Day of Atonement, and
means cessation or resting. This is the first use of the word
SABBATH in OT, though the idea occurs in Gen. 2.1-4. The
Israelites were to bake and boil as they pleased on Fridays, to
eat what they wanted, and to keep what was left over. Unlike
other days what was kept on Friday nights would not go
bad, but could be eaten on Saturdays, when no manna was
provided. Some venturesome spirits who went to look for
manna on Saturdays found none. The reproach of v. 28 occurs
a little later, or else the story falls after the giving of the ten
commandments in Ex. 20. The story implies that it was only
in connection with the manna that the Israelites discovered the
law of the Sabbath. IN HIS PLACE . . . OUT OF HIS PLACE Heb.
where he is . . . out of his place.

31. manna   The mystery of the substance is not only expressed
in its name; it is also likened to coriander seed—small round
grey-white seeds, or in Num. 11.7 to bdellium, a scented clear
gum. Also MANNA tasted like oil and honey pastry. Further,

so extraordinary was it that a jar containing about $6\frac{1}{2}$ pounds of it was to be laid up before God, before the Testimony, the Ark, in the Sanctuary, in perpetuity. Again a post-Sinai moment is in mind. The Israelites were to eat the MANNA for FORTY YEARS until they reached Canaan (Josh. 5.12).

MASSAH AND MERIBAH

17.1-7

P is found in 1, and J E in 2-7. These last six verses represent one of the most tangled and perplexing passages of Exodus, but nevertheless are also one of the pivotal points of the book. Discontent breaks out among the travellers because of lack of water. In reply Moses voices the questions: e.g. Why do you contend with me? Why do you test the Lord? The verbs 'contend' and 'test' correspond also to the meaning of the two place-names mentioned in 7, Massah (testing), and Meribah (contention). The two verbs 'contend' and 'test' occur again in 7, where the second verb is now directly linked to the question of the people which rounds off the passage 'Is the Lord among us or not?' In 6f. Horeb appears to be linked with Massah and Meribah.

A parallel story occurs in Num. 20.2-13, but here only one name, Meribah, is mentioned, and it is linked in Num. 20.1 with Kadesh. Massah and Meribah occur together in Deut. 33.8, and Ps. 95.8, no doubt reflecting this present passage in Exodus. In Deut. 6.16, and probably 9.22, Massah is mentioned without Meribah.

These are some of the facts which underlie one of the portions of this narrative.

(a) Some say that the stories in Ex. 17 and Num. 20 are simply variants.

(b) Others say there were once two stories, one centred on Massah, and another concerning Meribah, now joined in Ex. 17.

(c) Others go further and say that the present Meribah story in Num. 20 is J, then the Meribah story in Exodus is E, and the Massah parts in Ex. 17 would be J.

(d) If the Meribah water story is original in Num. 20, then the

Meribah story is post-Sinai, and it is a Kadesh story (Num. 20.1; 27.14; Deut. 32.51; Ezek. 47.19; 48.28), or a Horeb story (Ex. 17.6).

(c) If the Massah testing story is original in Ex. 17, then the Massah story is pre-Sinai (Rephidim, 17.1).

These are some of the facts and the problems of the passage. Clearly:

1. The question 'Is the LORD among us or not'? is the climax of the present story.

2. This question explains the Massah theme (so the verbs), or less likely the Meribah theme (so M. Noth).

3. This question may belong to the tradition in its present pre-Sinai setting, or if it belongs to the Meribah tradition of Num. 20, then it is post-Sinai.

4. Whether it is pre-Sinai or post-Sinai it points retrospectively to some teaching they have been given; it points to a teaching, an interpretation of their recent experiences in terms of the Presence of God. In short, Moses has imparted to them the belief, gained by himself at his call (3.12 etc.), that the meaning of his own life, his apostolic mission among them, and their deliverance from Egypt, is to be found in the faith that the Presence of God is among them.

If the Massah story is post-Sinai, then Moses could have imparted his conviction through the media of the events at Sinai, and the story must be removed to some such context as Num. 20 in order to follow the sojourn at Sinai. If the story is pre-Sinai, then Moses has already imparted his teaching of God's Presence to the Israelites in Egypt.

Provided that Massah may be separated from Meribah, then the Massah story is one of the keys to the Book of Exodus and a pivotal point and clue to the meaning of the book itself, and to the course of events in the book.

1. stages Lit. pluckings up, i.e. of breaking camp, and so

stages of a journey. REPHIDIM: location uncertain—it could
be in the upper parts of the Wâdī Feiran, but some way short
of the oasis of Wâdī Feiran. Others place it some 27 miles
beyond Feiran, others even nearer the traditional area of Sinai,
as the last stopping place before Sinai.

2. find fault   So RSV, but the Heb. is stronger—'dispute, contend, expostulate'. The double question in this verse reveals
both themes. In 3 RSV US . . . OUR. . . . OUR corresponds to
'me . . . my. . . . my' in Heb. THE ROD (v. 5) is Moses' shepherd's rod to which E is so partial. AT HOREB: all the commentators recognize this word as a difficulty here. The Israelites
are in Rephidim; but Horeb here belongs to the water-theme,
also to the Meribah theme; but Meribah is Kadesh and not
Sinai. Perhaps Horeb is a gloss here or else it describes not a
location but a great area.

VICTORY OVER AMALEK

17.8-16

Probably E.

The Amalekites, descendants of Amalek, grandson of Esau, are a bedouin people generally located (in the stories of the Judges, Saul and David) in the Negeb—southern Judah stretching towards the desert to the Kadesh area. These people attack the Israelites to prevent their advance into Amalekite territory and possibly to prevent Israel's seizure of the Feiran Oasis (near Rephidim), or if that is too far south, of the Kadesh Oasis itself. In the latter case the story would be post-Sinai corresponding to the picture of an elderly Moses who, seated, needed help to hold up his arms.

8. fought Amalekites are the aggressors and in Deut. 25.18 they also attack Israel's rear. Israel prepares for battle next day, and Joshua leads the army, possibly because Moses is too old. Joshua appears here for the first time, and often is described in the Pentateuch as Moses' attendant. Previously known as Hoshea, he was called Joshua first at Kadesh (Num. 13.8, 16).

THE HILL points to a definite locality, as does THE STONE of v. 12. THE ROD again points to E. HUR, only here and at Ex. 24.14—perhaps=a Horite, i.e. Hurrian, an Israelite leader and a deputy for Moses. The victory is said to depend upon Moses' strength—a mixture of magical elements and moral encouragement.

EDGE OF THE SWORD—lit. mouth of the sword; i.e. without quarter.

14. recite What is written in a book must also be learnt by heart by Joshua as a guide to God's mind and Israel's future attitude to Amalek. The double transmission emphasizes the importance of the subject matter.

15. an altar is erected, presumably used for a victory offering, and named, 'THE LORD IS MY BANNER'.

A HAND UPON THE BANNER ... RSV, according to a widely adopted emendation, has altered the Heb. which could be read 'A hand upon the throne of. . . .' . A HAND UPON may mean the lifting of the hand to express an oath.

MOSES' FATHER-IN-LAW VISITS HIM AT THE MOUNTAIN OF GOD

18.1-27 E

This chapter offers what is almost exclusively a piece of ancient E tradition (the end of vv. 1 and 8, with vv. 9-11, may be a J expansion). By 17.1 the Israelites are at Rephidim, and 19.1f. records the journey from Rephidim to Sinai. The events of ch. 18 should have taken place in the Rephidim wilderness, but 18.5 sets the scene at the mountain of God, i.e. Sinai. Clearly then the chapter is out of place, for it is a Sinai story recorded of some locality before they reach Sinai. This displacement is confirmed by the appearance of this story in Deuteronomy as a record of events at Sinai, but towards the end of the stay of the Israelites there. In Deut. 1.6-8 we find the divine direction to leave Horeb; in 1.19 they depart; Deut. 1.9-18 is the D parallel to the appointment of the law officers of Ex. 18.13-27.

This chapter records the visit of the Israelites to the mountain, where Jethro, the priest of Midian and Moses' father-in-law, also pays a visit. Jethro presides at the sacrifice, so the Israelites and the Midianite group celebrate a pilgrimage feast at a Midianite sanctuary, and Jethro presides at his own shrine. The next day he proposes to Moses new arrangements for the judicial life of the Israelite group. Moses accepts these and carries them out. The story is therefore important because it reveals Moses in the guise of an Israelite priest enacting judicial, ceremonial and ethical laws and precedents. Ch. 18. thus testifies to the very great importance of the Midianite shrine, with its God, the Lord, its priest, Jethro, and his sacrifices and legal directions for desert Israelites, even although the chapter may not justify the total acceptance of the so-called Kenite or Midian hypothesis, according to which Moses took over from Midian and Jethro their God, the Lord, and introduced him as a new god to the Israelites. Rather the chapter supports the view that Moses received a new revelation of the ancestral God of some Israelite groups, but underwent that experience among people who were both distantly related to the Israelites (through Abraham's second wife Keturah, the fourth of whose six sons was Midian, Gen. 25.1-6), and also had maintained some sort of faith in the Lord as their ancestral deity.

THE SACRIFICIAL MEAL

18.1-12

Jethro . . . heard . . . If there was any substance of fact in the stories of Ex. 1-15, the desert clans would soon have heard how a group of Israelites had successfully fled from Egypt in spite of all the Egyptians could do. Jethro, eager for a first-hand account, seeks out Moses at the mount. By 3.12 Jethro would have known Moses' destination. Jethro brings Moses' wife and two sons with him. 2.25 and 4.25 (J) speak of one son only, but time has elapsed and the fact of two sons only implies the separation of husband and wife and the consequent limitation of the family to only two sons, whose names are given and explained: Gershom as in 2.22, and Eliezer (My God is a help). SWORD OF PHARAOH occurs only here, but the reference could be to 2.15.

5. mountain of God According to 3.1 this is Horeb, and so the wilderness can only be the wilderness of Sinai, some distance from Rephidim. LO: Heb. reads 'I', but RSV follows LXX, Samaritan and Syriac in reading 'Behold', and thus reports the words of a messenger to Moses. DID OBEISANCE: lit. 'bowed himself down'—the correct and courteous behaviour to a father-in-law. The family scene in the open air serves also to

introduce the real heart of this tradition—Moses' report of the
deliverance from Egypt and the hardships of the journey, and
Jethro's joy and satisfaction. Then in v. 11 Jethro confesses
that the Lord is greater than all gods and goes on to preside
at the sacrificial meal. Jethro's confession could be the confession of the latest adherent to Yahwism, but more likely is
his joyous confirmation of a truth long known to him. Otherwise we must suppose the newest convert presided at the feast.
Aaron and the elders of Israel join Jethro in a meal before
God. Moses is not mentioned among the Israelite group. Presumably then he was numbered without being named among
the Midianite group. RSV has moved the last clause of v. 10
to be the penultimate clause of v. 11, in order to complete the
otherwise unfinished sense of v. 11. EAT BREAD means not that
they only ate bread but that the occasion was a sacrificial meal
at a shrine with an altar. The sacrifices would then be something akin to 'peace offerings'—sacrifice to God, and communion with God and with each other, through the meal.

APPOINTMENT OF ABLE MEN TO ADMINISTER JUSTICE

18.13-27

ON THE MORROW: Jethro observes the long and arduous duties
carried out by Moses in maintaining peace and friendship
among his followers by settling their disputes. Had Moses
appointed a periodic day for such pursuits? Moses settles the
disputes by reference to divine STATUTES, prescribed and
known decrees, and by giving decisions, *toroth*, directions of
all kinds, cultic and ethical, in the form of *ad hoc* pronounce-
ments. Jethro therefore suggests to Moses a lightening of his
labours, whereby Moses would deal only with difficult cases,
and the more trivial disputes could be settled by minor

officials. Moses is to REPRESENT THE PEOPLE BEFORE GOD, by
presenting their suits for divine intervention, so that Moses'
decisions have also the character and authority of a divine
discipline and education for the Israelites. Jethro also suggests
the selection of able, reverent, trustworthy men who are
beyond bribery, to serve as RULERS i.e. princes, or captains of
thousands, hundreds, fifties and tens, and to share Moses'
burden of legislative work. The actual words like captains and
the precise figures suggest a rather military organization and
may be a later expansion more accurately defining the number of the divisions. In the text the distinction is between
GREAT MATTERS and SMALL MATTERS, whereby the great
matters, because difficult, have to be referred to God, i.e. to
the sacred lot, etc. The passage may imply the beginning of
the distinction between sacral and ordinary civic law—*fas* and
jus.

24. SO MOSES GAVE HEED to the longer experience and greater
wisdom in such matters of his father-in-law. Moses reforms
his judicial work and keeps it that way. AND THEY JUDGED:
i.e. and they used to judge . . . they used to bring, and they
used to decide. The verbs of v. 26 are frequentatives.

27. Then Moses let . . . The Heb. may also suggest reluct-
ance on Moses' part, which confirms the picture of close
co-operation and warm cordiality between the two men. For
a season then Jethro withdraws from the Israelites, i.e. takes
his departure after a visit to them at the Mount, returning
to HIS OWN COUNTRY, that is, Midian. According to 3.1 and
18.27 some distance separates Jethro's home and the mount.

PART III

THE ISRAELITES AT SINAI
19.1-40.38

Chs. 19, 24, and 32-34 are mainly J E, 20-23 mainly E and 25-31 and 35-40 are P. Ch. 19 begins by recalling the arrival of the Israelites at Sinai, where they remain throughout the remainder of the Book of Exodus, and are only said to leave the mountain at Num. 10.11f. Ex. 19 sets the scene at Sinai, chs. 20-23 contain the Ten Commandments and the Book of the Covenant, ch. 24 records the ceremony of the Sinai Covenant. In chs. 25-31 the Priestly writers provide directions for the construction of the Tabernacle and the consecration of priests, and in chs. 35-40 relate how these directions were carried out. Chs. 32-34 tell the story of the Golden Calf and the consequences of that incident for these Israelites in the wilderness.

THE SCENE AT SINAI

19.1-25

19.3b-9, 11b-13, 18, 20-24 J; 19.2b-3a, 10-11a, 14-17, 19 E; 19.1-2a P. In 19.1-2a P records the arrival of the Israelites at Sinai, just as in his next statement (24.15b-18) he describes the settling of the divine glory on the mount. Then at God's command Moses delivers a charge to the Israelites (vv. 4-6), which the people accept (vv. 7-8), and goes on to promise a divine audition which is to accompany the Lord's visit to Moses (v. 9).

Still by divine command Moses prepares the people for the audition (vv. 10-15), and this now takes place in fire and smoke (vv. 16-20), and during the audition warnings concerning the approach to the mountain are first given (vv. 21-25).

In spite of certain difficulties concerning the precise position of Moses (cp. 19.3a with 3b etc.), certain doublets (19.2) etc., the general position is clear. Israel's arrival at Sinai is followed by a cloud theophany containing a series of auditions (cp. 19-24), in all of which Moses is involved both personally for himself and as mediator for his fellows.

1. ON THE THIRD NEW MOON (RSV) is better than IN THE THIRD MONTH of the EVV, because ON THAT DAY is then explained.

2. before the mountain The Israelites encamp before Mount Sinai. This mountain is traditionally identified with a granite ridge some two miles long, among the mountains in the apex of the Sinai Peninsula. This ridge ends in the north at the mountain Ras-es-safsafseh (6,937 feet) above the plain of Er Raha, about 5,000 feet above sea level and subject to intense cold, and in its southern end at Jebel Musa (7,363 feet) which is not visible from Er Raha. Jebel Musa is the more favoured

peak. Jebel Serbal some twenty miles away, and not far from
the Wâdī Feiran, is more isolated and imposing, and is
claimed as Sinai by others. Some scholars have pointed out
that Ex. 19.16, 18 require volcanic features as an explanation,
and such a volcanic mountain would have to be sought in the
area east and south of the Gulf of 'Akaba. Moses' call is also
placed at a mountain in or near Midian, i.e. in north-west
Arabia and east of 'Akaba (Deut. 33.2; Judg. 5.4f.). These
scripture references just quoted have suggested to yet other
scholars a third area for Sinai, namely among the mountains
of Kadesh, i.e. Kadesh Barnea, an oasis watered with three
springs some miles apart, at one of which, el Qudeirat, an
Israelite fort existed from the tenth to the eighth centuries.
But Deut. 1.2 says that it is a journey of eleven days from
Kadesh to Horeb, which is of course Sinai. The view adopted
here is that Israel journeyed from Egypt to Sinai in the
apex of the Sinai Peninsula, then left Sinai for Kadesh
where they spent thirty-eight years of their sojourn in the
wilderness before beginning to journey round Edom towards
Canaan. The visit to Sinai, whether in the Sinai apex or in
Midian, is an episode in the wilderness period. The tradition
of a three days' journey from Egypt into the wilderness does
not fit any of the three locations proposed for Sinai. Judg.
11.16 may suggest, though not necessarily, that Israel went
straight to Kadesh, but the Kadesh references in Ex. 16-18
probably belong to post-Sinai stories. Either the Israelites
went straight to Kadesh and after the stay at Sinai returned
to remain at Kadesh, or they went straight to Sinai (apex or
Midian) and then went on to remain at Kadesh. For the remainder of the Book of Exodus they were at Sinai.

3-6. And Moses went up   The events of Sinai begin with a
divine announcement mediated by Moses to the people. The
announcement recapitulates the deliverance from Egypt and
Israel's safe journey, like an eagle's flight, to the Lord's desert

home. Subject to their obedience and fidelity the Israelites, here styled the house of Jacob, are to be marked out as the Lord's people. Vv. 3b-6 present J's view of Israel as seen by God, and is certainly one of the great biblical passages 'on the nature and aim of the theocratic covenant' (Dillmann). Their obedient life in the covenant (24.3-8) will give the Israelites title at four points:

(a) They will be MY OWN POSSESSION. He is not to become theirs, but they are to become his particular, closely related and valuable POSSESSION or property. The Hebrew noun means 'specially one's own'.

(b) This relationship will be unique AMONG ALL PEOPLES and is grounded in the fact that the Lord is Lord of all the earth. This monotheistic affirmation based on a henotheistic fact requires a polytheistic background for its assertion. The affirmation is not too late in the days of the prophets, but it is not too early for the days of Moses.

(c) A KINGDOM OF PRIESTS: each member of this kingdom is a priest, with the right of access to the divine presence and with the gift of competence in that presence. The word kingdom is not to be pressed, and it is simply a synonym for a national unit.

(d) A HOLY NATION: a unique phrase—cp. 'holy people', often in Deut.—emphasizes not only the ethical character but also the divine axis of Israel. HOLY has a theistic reference meaning 'belonging to God', as well as a moral content. Some have seen in these verses the creed of a sanctuary, e.g. Gilgal.

This passage then sets forth the divine portrayal of the ideal Israel: unique, treasured, united, officiant among the nations, belonging to God. The passage probably combines two points of view. This newly constituted Israel is certainly to be the exemplar believing, behaving, worshipping community among the nations, the prototypal religious member in the community of the peoples, the theocratic focus of the Lord's purpose, and the mirrored reflection of his Presence (Ex. 33.16). But such a role carries with it the further thought that Israel is 'to bring other nations to the worship of God and to teach them his will' (McNeile). The priest among his people ministered to God and to the people. Israel among the nations ministers to God and then eventually to the peoples. This second role may not be explicit in the present passage but is implicitly and inevitably bound up in its general thought.

The thought of the passage, even if expressed in the categories of later days, marks a decisive stage in the development of the Book of Exodus. Up until now the Israelites, as the descendants of the patriarchs, as slaves in Egypt, as clans and families in need of deliverance and help, have been rescued by the Lord without condition or indeed consideration of any kind. Now that their deliverance is accomplished, the status must be defined, the relationship set forth. The Israelites, the sought after, are to become the covenanted, the committed. The engagement is to become a marriage, a covenant. Henceforth it will be embryonically possible to speak of Israel as well as of the Israelites.

7-9. ALL . . . WE WILL DO: the words testify to the optimism, enthusiasm and innocence of the speakers. LO, I AM COMING, i.e. about to come. The Lord, invisible in the clouds of Sinai, will address himself to Moses in such a way as to be overheard convincingly by the people.

10-15. Moses, having thus laid down the general conditions on both sides, is now instructed to express the situation in worship. Moses is to CONSECRATE his people; ritual ablutions, and continence (15b) are particularly enjoined. Holiness is to accumulate over three days in readiness for the divine appearance, and for the careful approach of the people to the mount. The mount, like its Lord, already possesses its holiness which is dangerous to all trespassers. Indeed any living thing, human or animal, that ventures on to the sacred territory must be destroyed by stoning or arrows, i.e. from a distance; the executioner must not step on to the mountain. THE TRUMPET: the blast of the ram's horn, used in Israel later to announce feast days, here bids the people approach the mount in readiness for the divine descent.

16-25. THE THIRD DAY: consecration is not only an act, but a process which extends into a third day when the right degree of fitness is attained. ON THE MORNING of this day, the mountain is shrouded in a thunderstorm of frightening severity (E). Moses brings his people to the foot of the mountain which is now described in terms of a volcano, a smoking, quaking cone (J). If v. 18 does describe a volcano, then it is difficult to understand how Moses got the people to take their stand and remain at the foot of a volcano in eruption. In such circumstances, and completely hidden, the Lord of Sinai descends upon the mountain. Sinai is not his dwelling place so much as his terrestrial manifestation point.

QUAKED GREATLY: Heb. and RSV have THE MOUNTAIN as the subject but LXX and some Heb. MSS have 'the people' as in 16b. THE TRUMPET in vv. 16, 19 and 20.18, is a different word from that used in 13b and in Josh. 6. The trumpet signalizes the Presence or advent of God as well as summons the people to attend. The verbs of v. 19 show that it is not a statement from each side, but a conversation which is being described. During the course of this conversation or to mark its end, God and Moses draw closer together (v. 20). God instructs Moses to curb any desire of the people to ascend (a volcanic mountain in eruption; cf. 20.18-20). Priests, who must also be consecrated, and people alike, are forbidden access. Indeed boundary marks have been set up to prevent trespass. But Moses is to go down and to return with Aaron, a direction which has no sequel. Moses went down . . . AND TOLD THEM (v. 25): this translation or paraphrase is probably incorrect. The Heb. says 'and he said to them', meaning that what was said,

namely the instructions of chs. 22f., would now follow. J
next appears in 24.1-2, 9-11. THE PRIESTS in v. 22 must either
be unofficial family ministers, or there must be some mistake,
for priests are not officially appointed as an order until
32.29.

THE TEN COMMANDMENTS

20.1-17 E

The narrative of events is suddenly interrupted by a speech of God announcing himself and his requirements. The first formulation of these requirements is found in 20.1-17, the Ten Commandments and a second formulation follows in 21.1-23.33, the so-called Book of the Covenant. At this point in the story, then, E has inserted two sets of divine requirements. These are not the composition of E, but are earlier, independent blocks of material incorporated by E in his story at this point.

INTRODUCTORY NOTE: EXODUS AND DEUTERONOMY

(a) In Exodus

1. They are orally revealed by God at 20.1, as ALL THESE WORDS.

2. In Deut. 4.13; 10.4 and probably Ex. 34.28 these words are described as the ten commandments, or words, written on two tables of stone.

3. In Ex. 31.18 the Priestly writer says that when God had finished his discourse with Moses, he gave Moses 'the two tables of the testimony, tables of stone written with the finger of God'.

4. In Ex. 32 Moses descends from the mountain after the episode of the Golden Calf carrying the tables of stone, and on seeing the calf he smashes the tables at the foot of the mountain.

5. In 34.1 Moses is said to prepare new blank tables of stone, to take them to the summit of the mount for the secret penmanship of God out of sight of the people.

The oral and written forms of the ten commandments are thus prior to the Golden Calf episode, that is, they are intended to belong to the making of the Covenant in Ex. 24. However, in view of 20.19, and because in 20.1ʹ the hearers of the divine speech are not stated, the commandments may not actually have reached the people until after the Golden Calf episode.

(b) *In Deuteronomy*

1. In Deut. 4.10 Moses gathers the Israelites to the foot of the mount, where they hear God's voice making known the covenant in the form of the ten commandments, which God then writes on stone tables. (cp. 5.4f. where Moses is the spokesman and intermediary).
2. In Deut. 9.9 Moses ascends the mountain and at the end of forty days on the mount receives the tables of stone, but smashes them after his descent from the mountain.
3. After a further period of forty days (9.25), Moses prepares the second set of stone tables for God's penmanship.
4. Moses also makes an ark and, after receiving the second set of tables, deposits them in this ark (10.1-5).

In the main, Deuteronomy confirms the Exodus account, but says explicitly that the Israelites had received the commandments at first orally, and then on the stone tables after the Calf incident, and adds the new information that the (second) pair of tables was stored in the ark.

It seems reasonable to conclude:
(a) that the ten commandments are prior to the Calf episode.
(b) that they belong to the theophany at Sinai (Ex. 19) and the making of the Covenant (24), which are the two great events at Sinai before the Calf episode (32).

Ex. 20 and Deut. 5.6-21 offer parallel versions of the Decalogue. The version in Deuteronomy differs from Ex. 20 mainly in offering a different reason for the observance of the Sabbath, and in reversing the order of house and wife in Ex. 20. Expansions which differ, as for the Sabbath commandment, suggest that the short form of the commandment without the expansion was original. All the commandments were short sentences, and their brevity would make for effect, for remembrance and for convenience. Their brevity would be all the more necessary if, as has been argued, the second of each of the two pairs of tables of stone was a copy of the first.

(c) The numbering of the ten commandments

20.1.-17 have been divided in different ways so as to yield ten laws.

(i) Jewish tradition has made 20.2 the first, and vv. 3-4 are then combined as the second commandment.

(ii) Some Christian traditions make vv. 3 and 4 the first, and read two commandments in v. 17.

(iii) It is probably best to make v. 2 a preface, v. 3 the first, vv. 4-6 the second commandment, and so on.

COMMENTARY

1. And God spoke all these words, saying This general statement must be understood in the light of the revelation promised in ch. 19 (19.9 J; 19.19 E).

The commandments are WORDS, words spoken by God. These divine words may then issue in salvation, promise, warning or law, but nevertheless all express divine grace. The motive, the spirit and the purpose of all God's words are always gracious.

2. I am the LORD your God, who brought you out of the land of Egypt Jewish tradition saw in the wonder and weight of these words the very first commandment prescribing belief in God, but these words are rather the authenticating preface to the commandments. Scholars like G. von Rad and M. Noth have argued that the Exodus and Sinai themes were originally distinct and unrelated. They argue this from the absence of references to Moses and the Sinai theme from the ancient summaries of Israel's faith known as Israel's credos (e.g. Deut. 4; Deut. 26; Josh. 24 etc.). In turn they see in this preface uttered at Sinai a linking of these originally separate themes. The two themes are sometimes further described in terms of Gospel and Law—redemptive act and then the commandments. G. E. Mendenhall's study of Hittite treaties, *Law and Covenant in Israel and the Ancient Near East*, has supplied a corrective to this divisive interpretation. From these treaties he shows that Hittite covenant forms supply a parallel to what is presented in Ex. 20 and in Deuteronomy. In these treaties the overlord, the head of the minor rulers, sets forth the relationship between himself and his vassals. He first proclaims his identity, then recapitulates the benefits he has conferred upon his vassal, and goes on to state the duties he requires from his vassal, the first of which is naturally an exclusive loyalty, and concludes with formulae of curses and blessings. Such treaties are then to be laid up in the vassal's temple and are to be periodically read in public. Just as the Book of Deuteronomy can be regarded as an expanded treatment of this covenant form, so Ex. 19-24 is another illustration, though without the curses and blessings feature.

Closer analysis of 20.2f. shows that this verse is the joining not of two themes—Deliverance and Law—but of three:

(*a*) The name theme, the revelation of the name of God by way of self-predication, is a mountain theme (cp. Ex. 3 and 34).

(*b*) WHO BROUGHT YOU OUT, the deliverance theme, is the Exodus out of Egypt theme.

(*c*) The commandments: the giving of the law took place at the mountain. So the deliverance theme figures between two features of the Sinai theme, and moreover they are in the right chronological order: the Name, the Deliverance, and the Law. Further the name controls each of the second and third themes equally—the manifestation of the Name means deliverance for Israel, and then means law for Israel, just as later in the book the name will spell itself out in divine guidance (23.20f.) and God's presence among his people (29.45f.). God will be what he will be—Revealer—Deliverer—Lawgiver—Guide—Presence. There is no division of grace and law. Deliverance and commandments are alike saving and educational. God's law is gospel, and God's gospel is law.

The First Commandment

3. You shall have no other gods before me   The person in the Heb. is singular throughout all the commandments. Other gods as alternatives, substitutes or extras are prohibited. Indeed they became impossible in real Yahwism. This is the first and fundamental principle of Yahwism. The verse implies both henotheism and a penumbra of polytheism, but is in itself a practical monotheism with the inevitability of an absolute monotheism. Nevertheless an absolute element exists in the words BEFORE ME, Heb. 'before', or 'against, beside, over, my face'. Where God's face is no other god may be present. If 'before my face' had originally a cultic reference implying some imageless token of God's presence, like the ark or the tent, then the prohibition would have a physical reference. What 'before me' means is uncertain, but a sinister nuance has been detected in the word 'before'. The prohibition preserves the solity ('only-ness') and by implication the unity of Israel's God.

The Second Commandment

4-6. You shall not make yourself a graven image . . .   This prohibition probably forbids the making of an image of the true God for use in worship, rather than images of all gods, who are not mentioned in these words, and rather than the prohibition of ornamental art in general. In this prohibition of all idolatrous worship, (but of all idolatry in general according to others), the Lord is preserved from containment in an image, and thus from the thought of control by the worshipper. His Presence and his power cannot be contained or controlled in any way, and so this prohibition is closely related to the Presence theology.

A GRAVEN IMAGE: of wood or stone with sometimes a metal covering. Perhaps the word implies a human form, but the expansion OR ANY LIKENESS excludes all shapes. The prohibition is intended to be absolute and so includes both living, angelic, birdlike, human, animal and fish forms, and inanimate forms in all three parts of the ancient universe. The last three clauses of v. 4 after the first prohibition, and vv. 5f., are probably expansions by way of explanation and justification. Israelites must not prostrate themselves before images. The Lord is JEALOUS: the word means 'hot, fiery, zealous'. The word 'jealous' sounds unworthy in modern ears, but it denotes a quality of enthusiastic and zealous concern for self which would be wrong in anybody except God. In the Old Testament the word is used in contexts where the solity ('only-ness'), unity or distinctive character of Israel's God is threatened or compromised. The word is the antidote to idolatry.

VISITING . . . the expansion now wanders from the precise prohibitions of image worship to the more general consequences of iniquity and obedience. The Hebrew participles translated VISITING . . . SHOWING . . . reveal liturgical formulae which contrast the limits put to divine punishment with the innumerable hosts—THOUSANDS—who enjoy God's covenant love and favour.

WHO LOVE AND KEEP—just as gospel and law express the divine attitude equally, and are not to be opposed, so love and obedience equally express the Israelite joy in God, and they are not to be separated or contrasted.

The older commentators thought this commandment was sure proof that the Decalogue could not be Mosaic, because images were a feature of Israel's worship in later times. Three comments are pertinent. The prohibition of images, like that of murder, does not mean that there were no images and no murders in later Israel. Secondly, most of the major images, like the Ark or Jeroboam's golden bulls, are really platforms for the invisible Presence of Israel's God, but some images there may well have been. On the other hand, and thirdly, archaeological remains have not yet yielded any certain images of Israel's God.

The Third Commandment

7. You shall not take the name of the LORD your God in vain Recalling the frequency and prominence of the theme of the divine Name in the Book of Exodus, the safeguarding of this Name in the commandments is not surprising. The commandment asserts the independence of the divine Name, and excludes its use or mention in vain, i.e. for any unreal or frivolous purpose, especially for perjury, false oaths and for private purposes of gain or magical control. Images of God are forbidden—but his Name is made known and will be used in worship and vows and therefore must be protected. HOLD GUILTLESS: i.e., leave unpunished.

The Fourth Commandment

8. Remember the sabbath day to keep it holy Deut. 5.12 reads 'Observe'. The expansion in Deuteronomy is longer because of some added details, but the motivation is quite different. In Exodus the motive for observance is the example of God, who in creation did all his work in six days and then blessed

and hallowed the seventh day. In Deuteronomy observance is
a memorial of Israel's deliverance from Egypt by God. Common to both accounts are the cessation of work, the holiness
of the day, and the fact that the day is a sabbath to the Lord.
REMEMBER means 'Be aware of', so that every seventh day is
marked out as a day belonging to the Lord. The origin of the
sabbath is unknown, but the earliest references, Amos 8.5;
Kings 4.23; Ex. 16.22-30, show that no work was done on that
day. Perhaps it began simply as a divine day in which no work
was done. It was early associated with the day of new moon, but
new moon and sabbath are mentioned together because they
are sacred days, and not because sabbath was also connected
with the moon.

SABBATH is a Heb. word meaning 'to cease', 'cessation', but
the original reference is not only disputed but unknown. The
social emphasis so prominent in Deuteronomy is also present
in Exodus, where all human beings and domesticated animals
are to share in the rest. Contrary to much argument, the keeping of such a day is possible in nomadic communities. This
commandment like the foregoing is related to God, and its
aim is to maintain the reality of the sense of God.

The Fifth Commandment

12. Honour your father and mother   The first four commandments embrace the duties to God—the fifth lays down the
importance of parents as next to God and as of course the
nearest neighbour. This is the first commandment with a
promise (Eph. 6.2), namely, long life; and similarly to curse
parents is to incur the death penalty (Lev. 20.9; 24.15f.). To
respect parents is a form of piety and in Deuteronomy brings
prosperity as well as long life. The commandment is not for
the young only, but for all whose parents are alive. To honour
parents is to maintain family life and so strengthen society,
but the reverse destroys family and society. Moses in his

bearing to his wife's father fulfils this commandment (Ex. 18.7).

The Sixth Commandment

13. You shall not kill This word forbids all killing, meditated and premeditated, but other texts suggest that the slaughter of animals, authorized slaying by the community, or the slaying (smiting) of enemies are outside the scope of this commandment. Inevitably the prohibition raises deeper questions, for, since God is the author of life, it follows that to take away life is to act in God's stead. This is where the problem begins. Jesus spiritualized this and the following commandments. Augustine claimed that suicide was included in this prohibition.

The Seventh Commandment

14. You shall not commit adultery This prohibition preserves marriage, forbids marital infidelity and probably includes the betrothed as well as the wife of another man. Death is the punishment (Lev. 18.20; 20.10; Deut. 22.22; Matt. 5.27f.).

The Eighth Commandment

15. You shall not steal The reference could be limited to property (but cp. the last commandment), but since in the context sins against persons are prohibited, the prohibition could include the theft of persons, kidnapping, enslaving, loss of liberty and so on (cp. Ex. 21.16; 22.1).

The Ninth Commandment

16. You shall not bear false witness against your neighbour

This prohibition insists upon the truth in all judicial processes. The neighbour is anybody with whom you have dealings.

BEAR FALSE WITNESS: lit. answer; to testify as a false witness. So by extension the words mean to make false statements about others.

The Tenth Commandment

17. You shall not covet your neighbour's house Perhaps it was originally: Do not covet, in the practical sense: You shall not attempt to acquire. HOUSE means probably 'everything he has', and does not imply a building, or life in Canaan. Deut. reverses the order and puts wife before house, possibly as showing a more humane spirit. The covetous acquisition presupposes covetous greed, and the prohibition may be levelled against the inward spirit as well as the outward act. By extension this prohibition could refer to a great deal of what is nowadays styled: 'keeping up with the Joneses'.

YOU SHALL NOT COVET: the second occurrence of these words, with what follows, is not a further separate commandment, as is often claimed, but explains the word 'house' as the first part of the verse.

CONCLUDING NOTE

The foregoing commandments seek to set forth right behaviour to God and to fellow men. The brief but basic stipulations are so comprehensive that they amount to a charter, a summary of spiritual behaviour. Their negative form only emphasizes their positive principles. Their distinction lies not only in their ethical excellence but in their theocratic character and divine origin. The commandments have the form of a

categorical revelation grounded in and yet setting forth the
covenant relationship. Accordingly they are so general as to
be timeless, and beyond legal or cultural or cultic reference.
Their genius lies in their assembly and in the collocation of
duties to God and to men. Increasingly their pre-prophetic
origin is being recognized, and this points to Mosaic thinking.
Another mind no less great saw in them the summary of all
behaviour and set them forth in his two commandments:
'Thou shalt love God. . . . Thou shalt love thy neighbour' (Mark 12.28-34). Though neither of these is in the
Ten Commandments, together they summarize and crown
them.

THE FEAR OF THE PEOPLE

20.18-21

These verses resume the last E verse, in Ex. 19.19, interrupted
by the insertion of the Decalogue, which would have been
more suitably placed at 20.20. YOU SPEAK TO US. The people
are so frightened that they request Moses to act as intermediary whilst they stand afar off. This demand contrasts with
the warning to the people in 19.21-25 not to come near the
mount. TO PROVE YOU—put you to the proof, i.e., whether you
will be obedient (cp. 16.4).

This difference in the story may be due to different authors,
J in 19 and E in 20. Nevertheless the discrepancy in the
attitude of the people remains, and the double authorship does
not solve the difficulty. Perhaps, then, two groups of people
were present here who behaved in different ways; those
who knew the limits of the sanctuary mountain and would
therefore not go near it, such people as the Kenites or
desert denizens; and others, strangers to the place, the fugitives
from Egypt, who did not know the holy limits, and had to

be warned to keep out and off. If two different groups of
people are here present, then the historic basis of the covenant
is forthcoming—the union of the Israelites from Egypt with
desert elements, or even their desert cousins, in a new
religious association under the Lord.

THE BOOK OF THE COVENANT

20.22-23.33

This section is usually entitled the Book of the Covenant from the occurrence of these words in 24.7, the book in which the covenant of Ex. 24 was enacted. This section is probably a separate code of Hebrew law, inserted between the theophany of 19 and the covenant ceremony of 24, as the oldest account, next to the Decalogue, of what was given to Moses on the mount.

The Book begins with some laws relating to worship, 20.22-26. Then 21.1, which marks at least a new heading, introduces various communal and criminal laws entitled 'judgments' or ORDINANCES 21.2-22.17. Different from the judgments which are in the form of common law, and state cases (i.e. they begin with such words as 'when', 'if', 'whoever') are the 'words' which express commands and prohibitions, and occur in the form YOU SHALL NOT. These words are found in 20.23-26 and, with exceptions, in 22.18-23.19. The code concludes in a sermonic addition concerned with the mode of the Presence of God with Israel on the way to Canaan and in that land, and which links the code to life in Canaan. (See Driver's Commentary, pp. 202-5, for contents and character of the code.)

The central part of the code, 21.1-23.19, also presupposes the way of life of an agricultural community. The code may then well contain single laws from the desert, other laws from the days of Israel's settlement in Canaan, and still others from Israelite and Canaanite life in that land over a long period back to the days of the patriarchs. Nevertheless any consideration of Ex. 20-23 must take account of the story of Moses' legislative work preserved in Ex. 18. The 'words' mentioned above could be Moses' work. The assembly of all the diverse laws in a code is certainly pre-Deuteronomic, probably premonarchical, and it has been suggested that this Book of the Covenant was associated once with the God of the Covenant known to be the God of Shechem. This law code would then be the code of ancient Shechem (Josh. 24.25).

The code is the earliest Israelite-Canaanite code of laws and takes its place in the series of ancient Near Eastern law codes that have come to light in the last century. Each code must be interpreted in the light of its own cultural context, for it represents an independent if parallel expression of the legal needs of the society in which it arose. No single law in Exodus, for example, exactly reproduces laws from the ancient code of Hammurabi, with which the Book of the Covenant is often compared. The connection is especially illustrated in the Judgments—in those laws expressed in the 'if' and 'when' forms—the casuistic laws so called.

REGULATIONS RELATING TO WORSHIP

20.22-23

In view of the quite separate beginning stated in the opening of 21.1, 'Now these are . . .', and which relates to what follows, the regulations relating to worship in 20.22-26 could be said to fall outside the main Book of the Covenant proper. Perhaps these laws should be related to other worship laws in 22.29f. and 23.10-19 as the separated remains of an early collection of laws relating to worship. Vv. 22b-23 are plural address, but vv. 24-26 are singular.

On the other hand the references to gods of gold (20.23), the altar (v. 24), the nakedness (v. 26), are strongly reminiscent of features of the golden calf story, so 22-26 may possibly be some *ad hoc* prescriptions relating to that incident. Both Exodus and Deuteronomy show that the golden calf incident took place somewhere between the giving of the Decalogue orally, and Moses' descent from the mount with the tables of stone. The order of events can no longer be ascertained. It remains a problem why the altar laws appear outside the Book of the Covenant.

YOU HAVE SEEN: these words are designed to authenticate the laws that follow, and are parallel to the opening words of 21.1. FROM HEAVEN: the words are emphatic by position in Heb., and virtually mean 'from above', i.e. from Sinai, from on and above Sinai, and higher than that!

You shall not make gods of silver to be with me The Heb. is different: 'You shall not make with me; gods of silver and gods of gold you shall not make for yourselves.' RSV has simply altered the punctuation. WITH ME is of course the equivalent of 'before me', or before my face in 20.3. This means to be associated with me (in the mind or attitude of the worshipper), or, preferably, 'beside me' (in the sanctuary). The words prohibit images of any god, and silver and gold probably refer to the gold and silver plated idols of the Canaanites so often found in Canaan.

THE ALTAR LAWS

20.24-26

Most of the law codes begin with altar or sanctuary laws (25.8; Deut. 12; Ezek. 40.5ff.). Altar-building is part of the theology of theophany. First God appears to mark out a place; at that place the altar must be erected and sacrifices offered. The spot so marked is the place where God makes known his name, so that altars recall the visitation by God. They continue then to be the places of this Presence and from them (priestly) blessings are pronounced.

ALTAR: lit. 'place where you slay'. Various features of these

laws, such as (*a*) simplicity of altars (a pile of earth, a heap
of stones untouched by tools); (*b*) the possibility of many
altars (IN EVERY PLACE); (*c*) that YOU (Israelites, not priests)
MAY SACRIFICE—all these features show the antiquity of the
prescriptions. Such simple altars permit the blood of the
sacrifices to drop to the ground easily. SACRIFICE—lit. 'slay'—
the same word as the word for altar. The two most common
kinds of sacrifice are:

(*a*) BURNT OFFERINGS: what goes up—what was completely
burnt on the altar. Cazelles has claimed this sacrifice as
stemming from Israel's patriarchs, but this is uncertain.

(*b*) PEACE OFFERINGS: probably sacrifices making for
fellowship between the god and his worshippers. The altar
retained certain parts but the rest was consumed by the
offerers. RSV suggests that the act of God in recording his
name follows the sacrifice. It is of course prior to sacrifice,
and is synonomous with the initial act of theophany. Likewise
the act of blessing is the outcome of the entire process, and
is the last element in the worship. IT (twice in v. 25b) refers to
STONE and not ALTAR. BY STEPS—these open air altars were
not even to be provided with steps lest heads of families in
short tunics should expose themselves. Later with stepped
altars the priests wore suitable garments (28.42).

JUDGMENTS

21.1-22.17

RSV ORDINANCES renders Heb. *mishpatim*—i.e. the sayings or decrees of a judge, precedents for further decisions in the form of case law. McNeile and others claim that the code is set forth in groups of five laws, but this is not always apparent.

RIGHTS OF HEBREW SLAVES

21.2-11

HEBREW is not necessarily ethnic but means a particular and probably a depressed social class.

These verses are a good example of the form of these laws. The fundamental principle is introduced by WHEN (21.2, 7, 20, 22 etc.), but the lesser clauses are introduced by IF (3a, 3b, 4, 5, 8, 9, 10, 11 etc.). Slavery, by reason of poverty, bankruptcy, sale or birth, was a normal feature of ancient Israelite life, but it is regulated by these laws. SIX YEARS: duration of enforced slavery is limited for single males to six years. The year of Jubilee (each fiftieth year) could further shorten the period, if it fell before the sixth year. FREE: a social term indicating a status higher than slavery but short of a full free Israelite.

3-4. single Lit. with his back, or his body—a legal term only here.

5. plainly says Better 'affirms'. The process is marked by several stages. (*a*) A visit to God, i.e. to the sanctuary, for the slave's formal declaration of the vow in the words given by RSV in quotation marks. The words are the actual legal

175

formula which had to be pronounced before witnesses at a shrine so as to prevent enforced or false declarations. (*b*) After the return home, the slave must stand at the threshold to mark his desire to belong to the household, and a hole is bored in the slave's ear, as the organ of obedience, and to show the master's acceptance of the life-long voluntary service.

7. sells his daughter The lot of (Israelite) girls sold to slavery is different from that of men, and also depends on the nature of the sale. A girl sold unconditionally must remain a slave. Vv. 8-11 probably go further than v. 7, as indicating sale with a view to concubinage or even marriage, and this status was doubtless the lot of the great majority. As a concubine further rights accrue to her.

FOR HIMSELF: emphatic by position in Heb. and contrasted with FOR HIS SON in v. 9. BE REDEEMED by her next of kin acting for the family. DEALT FAITHLESSLY i.e. in not carrying out the conditions of the sale and marrying her to himself. HER FOOD: lit. her flesh, i.e. ration of meat.

11. these three things Either the three things of v. 10, or the three ways of dealing with her, namely, marrying her himself; letting her be redeemed and be married to another Israelite; letting his son marry her.

CAPITAL OFFENCES

21.12-17

Whoever The law is participial in form and both alliteration and construction are striking. The Heb. is: *Makeh 'ish wameth, moth yumath.* 'He who smites a man and he dies shall surely be done to death.' Probably not the state but the

next of kin of the victim exacted the penalty. V. 13 provides
for unpremeditated murder; such unintentional slayers could
take refuge at a place, i.e. an altar (v. 14), or other place of
asylum (cp. Deut. 4.41 etc.). BUT GOD LET HIM FALL: i.e., if he
kills him accidentally. The striking or cursing of parents or
the kidnapping of a man are also punished by death.

14. another Lit. 'his neighbour', i.e. anyone whom a man
meets in daily life (Ex. 20.17).

16. sells him probably to foreigners.

BODILY INJURIES NOT RESULTING IN DEATH

21.18-36

Injuries by men, vv. 18-27; by animals, vv. 28-32; due to
negligence, vv. 33-36. None of these cases involved death, and
so the purpose of the laws is to provide for compensation
according to the sex and status of the injured.

18. fist So LXX and this is preferable to spade, hoe or club
which are possible meanings. RISES AGAIN, i.e., is convalescent
and recovering. The assailant must then as in other law codes
pay compensation for lying up or injury time, and HAVE HIM
THOROUGHLY HEALED, i.e. pay his doctor's bill.

20. When a man strikes his slave In 12 a man who kills a
man is PUT TO DEATH, i.e. a life for a life, but here a man who
kills a slave is only PUNISHED: lit. 'avenged'. If by being
avenged is meant the death of the slayer, then 20 agrees with
13. Otherwise if a fine is envisaged, then the slave is of less
value than a man, and so he who slays a slave does not
forfeit his life. Indeed if an owner only wounds his slave, and

the slave recovers after a day or two, then the owner did not
mean to kill him and goes scot free, i.e. he has been punished
in the loss of the slave's time and work. HIS MONEY: i.e., his
property.

22. hurt a woman with child   a pregnant woman in a circle
of onlookers is accidentally hurt as the fighters thrash about;
perhaps such a woman intervened to help her husband or
relative. The woman's husband decides the amount of
damages and this amount is further approved by the judges.

AS THE JUDGES: with change of one consonant the text
could be read 'and he shall pay for the miscarriage', this
emendation would mean that the husband could fix his own
compensation, but the reading JUDGES is better and more in
accord with justice.

23-25. MISCHIEF means of course the death of the woman, and
this leads us to a passage not closely related to 20f., setting
forth the *lex talionis*, the doctrine that the punishment must
fit the crime. An EYE FOR AN EYE is the law of revenge and
therefore not a very spiritual doctrine. On the other hand in
the history of punishment, it represents a great step forward
—for it limited the punishment to the exact equivalent of the
crime. In earlier times Lamech, for example, had killed a man
for a wound and exacted a seventy-seven-fold vengeance
(Gen. 4.23f.).

26-27. When a man, however, injures his own slave, the eye
for eye law does not apply. The owner does not lose his own
eye or tooth, but has to release the slave and so lose his
services. The slave is valued less than a free man.

28-32. A goring ox is to be stoned to death. Its flesh may not
be eaten because blood guilt attaches to it and renders it
taboo. But in certain circumstances of negligence the owner of

the ox could be put to death, though the relatives of the
person gored to death could agree to a ransom and thus save
the life of the ox's owner. RANSOM: the price of a life. The
same law applied to a minor (31). For the death of a slave the
ox's owner paid thirty silver shekels, the ox being slain. The
verse thus indirectly shows the market price of a slave.

33-36. Animals who fall into pits or wells must be compen-
sated for. Perhaps SHALL MAKE IT GOOD meant at one time
the handing over of an equivalent beast; then money was paid
in compensation and the defaulter kept the dead animal for
its hide and food value (but cp. Deut. 14.21; Lev. 17.15f.).
Injury to animals by animals must be borne equally by the
owners, unless one owner had been negligent, in which case
it was ox for ox, and the dead beast could be kept.

THIEVING AND DAMAGE

22.1-6

RSV rightly reads the verses in the order 1, 3b, 4, 2, 3a.
FIVE OXEN—oxen as draught animals were more valuable
than sheep and were more liable to be stolen. Restitution was
five oxen for a stolen, slain ox, but only four sheep for a
similar sheep. (cp. II Sam. 12.4-6). FOR HIS THEFT (v. 1=v.
3b): i. e., not as a punishment for stealing but as compensation for what was stolen.

HE SHALL PAY DOUBLE: i.e., he is to return the stolen beast
or its equivalent, and then hand over a second beast or its
equivalent as a fine.

2. breaking in Lit. digging through, i.e. the walls. FOR HIM
(v. 2) means 'for the householder'. UPON HIM and FOR HIM in
v. 3 refer to the thief and the householder respectively. The

householder who kills a thief in the dark suffers no guilt,
because the intruder may have intended burglary or murder.

5-6. The interpretation of the Hebrew verb, GRAZED OVER,
and the different values of restitution are difficult. Two ex-
pedients have been adopted.

(*a*) Driver with slight alterations gives the more usual
meaning to the verb. If A MAN CAUSES A FIELD OR A VINEYARD
TO BE burnt and lets the burning spread and it burns IN
ANOTHER MAN'S FIELD. . . . This reading makes the burning
of v. 5 deliberate and receives heavier punishment—the BEST
IN HIS OWN FIELD must be given up; whereas the burning in
v. 6 is accidental, and so only FULL (i.e. equivalent) restitution
must be made.

(*b*) After ANOTHER MAN'S FIELD in v. 5, add from LXX
and Samaritan 'he shall surely make it good from his own
field according to its produce, but if it eat the whole of the
field'. . . . If the whole of the field is eaten, then, (*a*) the
negligence was greater because it lasted longer, and (*b*) no
evidence of the quantity of the eaten crop remains—so the
responsible party must make restitution from the best of his
own crop. Commentators are divided between the two solutions, but the first involves some slight emendation of the
text.

GOODS OR ANIMALS DEPOSITED WITH A
NEIGHBOUR FOR SAFE KEEPING

22.7-13

These laws introduce a further complication. What happens
when a man asks his neighbour to take care of his goods or
beasts, during temporary absence, and such deposited property
disappears or is damaged? Clearly guilt may lie in one or two

places—a thief may be responsible without the knowledge of the temporary caretaker; but if the thief is not found then the caretaker himself may be responsible. The further case of a conspiracy is not mentioned. In such doubtful cases resort is made to religion, and the unknown is resolved by recourse to the fear of the greater unknown by means of oaths and curses at the sanctuary. The innocent caretaker would not be affected by any curse laid upon him, but if he is guilty, then the curse would be effective and reveal his guilt. The law of v. 7b is matched by a general principle in v. 9, which is very ancient.

HE WHOM GOD SHALL CONDEMN is, because of the plural Heb. verb, more rightly translated as HE WHOM THE GODS CONDEMN, and this shows the pre- or non-Israelite origin of the direction.

This is it A man may lose something, and an identical but not necessarily the same object may be found in another's possession. Again there is a doubt which is not resolvable and recourse must be made to the processes of the sanctuaries.

10-13. For animals entrusted to a neighbour the law is the same as for deposited goods, except that animals may die, or be hurt as well as be stolen. The doubt now is whether the caretaker has slain or hurt the animals, and so they commit themselves to the ordeal of an oath by the Lord. The use of the word Lord here rather than God (so LXX) probably shows that the law is genuinely Israelite.

is driven away Probably an accidental duplication of the preceeding Heb. verb, which only differs by one letter. V. 12 deals with the case of the animal driven off, i.e. STOLEN. SHALL ACCEPT THE OATH: since the result of the oath is inevitable, it has been claimed that the words mean the owner of the animal shall accept it back dead or hurt, and the caretaker will pay no compensation.

But if it is stolen   Restitution must be paid because negligence of the caretaker is partly responsible for the theft.

If it is torn by beasts   If the herdsman or caretaker can produce a part of the torn beast, then that proves he was on the alert, and so restitution is not called for (cp. I Sam. 17.35; Amos 3.12).

BORROWING

22.14-15

If a man borrows   The Heb. does not state an object but the next clause shows that an animal is meant. NOT BEING WITH IT—if the owner had been present then he would have prevented the hurt or slaying of the beast. In the absence of the owner the borrower must compensate for the loss of the animal.

IF IT WAS HIRED IT CAME . . . could refer to the beast. If the beast WAS HIRED, then the hirer was prepared for the loss of the beast, i.e., no compensation. But the word HIRED usually means a hired servant, who would then have to pay for loss or damage in respect of any animal entrusted to him by his master, and injured while it was in the servant's care. Such compensation would be taken out of his hiring charge.

RAVISHING OF AN UNBETROTHED VIRGIN

22.16-17

A man who seduces an unbetrothed virgin must put matters right by marrying the girl, and paying the marriage present or price to her father. If, however, the father does not consent

to the marriage, then he still receives the marriage price as
compensation for damage to his property—i.e. his daughter.
The Book of the Covenant does not contain a section dealing
with marriage laws (cp. Deut. 22.13-26), and the case of the
ravished virgin figures here in the property laws, so the real
point again is the amount of compensation, and not the rights
of the girl or the sanctity of marriage itself. In Deut. 22.28 for
rape the amount of compensation is 50 shekels of silver, about
£7. Assyrian law fixed the compensation as three times the
value of the marriage price. To seduce a betrothed virgin is of
course adultery (cp. Deut. 22.23ff.).

PROHIBITIONS AND COMMANDMENTS

22.18-23.19

A collection of prohibitions and commandments in the 'You shall (not)' form. This is the so-called apodeictic law, but the prohibitions are not systematically arranged and there are explanatory additions. They prohibit specific evils and enjoin specific duties, and so are very different from the hypothetical laws in the 'when' and 'if' forms of 21.1-22.17. Generally speaking 22.18-23.19 illustrate more keenly the spirit and genius of Israel's religion.

THREE CAPITAL OFFENCES

22.18-20

You shall not permit a sorceress to live The Hebrew verb used in this passage means 'to put to the ban', to 'devote', to exterminate, and describes what was done to peoples, cities and things regarded as hostile to Israel's God. Josh. 6.17-20 is an illustration of the working of this principle of extermination, whereby all the inhabitants of Jericho with exceptions were to be slain, and all its metal confiscated and given to 'the treasury of the Lord'.

HUMANE DUTIES

22.21-27

A group of laws designed to protect the resident alien, the widow, the orphan and the poor in general.

stranger A resident alien—somebody who does not belong to

a district or to the people living in that district, but who nevertheless resides in that district and among those people. He
is different from a foreigner and from a stranger, but as
resident has certain rights of hospitality. He must not be
exploited, FOR YOU WERE STRANGERS: the explanatory addition reminds Israel of her status in Egypt—an addition quite
in the Deuteronomic spirit (cp. 23.9). Vv. 23f. are again an
expansion, and like v. 27 show how God himself is concerned
for the under-privileged. Vv. 25-27 reveal an interesting for-
mation. The two basic phrases are (a) the prohibition: YOU
SHALL NOT BE TO HIM AS A CREDITOR (explained by the rest
of v. 25 as a prohibition of taking interest from a fellow
Israelite), and (b) the command: YOU SHALL RESTORE IT TO
HIM. These two clauses have been set in a context of 'if'
clauses—as if they were common law cases. Loans were
normally for the relief of poverty, and to take interest on such
loans would be wicked. GARMENT, i.e., the outer garment in
which a person slept. To retain such a garment given in pledge
would be to subject the owner of the garment to the cruelty of
cold nights, unless the need of the person to whom the garment
had been pledged was greater (cp. Deut. 24.12).

The verbs change from plural to singular and back again
and the changes point to additions.

THE RIGHTS OF GOD

22.28-31

28. revile God . . . curse a ruler REVILE and CURSE are here
virtually synonymous. The word for RULER is not king but
nasi, a prince, a word found only in Priestly diction in the Old
Testament (P, Ezekiel and Chronicles). A *nasi* is lit. one lifted
up, one who bears rule. The term probably supposes the

pre-monarchic tribal organization of Israel and designates a
representative or even spokesman of the clan.

29-31. Customary offerings and renunciations.

FULNESS: of corn; OUTFLOW: lit. juice, i.e., of wine and
oil. First fruits are probably intended, and this would agree
with the demand for the dedication of first-born of men and
animals in v. 30. The first-born of oxen and sheep were to be
offered ON THE EIGHTH DAY—this would limit the choice of
lamb available for Passover. V. 31 is probably a later addition.
Israelites are holy and are therefore not to eat meat which
has not been killed in a holy way, i.e., by having its blood
drained.

ISRAELITE PROBITY AND COMPASSION

23.1-9

Vv. 1-3, 6-9 are apodeictic but vv. 4f. combine case law and
commandments. The apodeictic verses presuppose the existence of the powerful rich and the helpless poor (v. 7), and are
designed to preserve impartiality in the courts in the face of
such social conditions.

a false report   Cp. 20.16. This covers both making up a false
report and circulating one. FALSE: lit. groundless.

join hands   A ceremonial of covenant, meaning 'to make common cause'.

2. follow a multitude   Be swayed by or give in to a multitude.
JUSTICE: this last word is not in the Hebrew but RSV adds
it from LXX.

3. poor man   Since v. 3 is virtually repeated in v. 6, most commentators read 'great' or 'powerful one' for POOR MAN in 3.

4-5. Right behaviour is due to an enemy—one who hates you or is even at law with you. (Cp. Deut. 22.1-4.) The Israelite must restore the straying beast and even more pointedly help his enemy to raise the ass fallen beneath its load. The Heb. of Ex. 23.5b is difficult; RSV follows Deut. 22.4.

6-9. There must be proper administration of justice to Israel's poor and the resident alien.

YOUR POOR: only here and Deut. 15.11.

DO NOT SLAY: if the false charge concerned a capital offence, then conspiracy could lead to the execution of the innocent.

I WILL NOT ACQUIT: LXX, thou shalt not justify . . . .

OFFICIALS: lit. the open-eyed—cp. Deut. 16.19, which has 'the eyes of the wise'. . . . SUBVERTS THE CAUSE: Heb. 'the words of the righteous.'

You shall not oppress a stranger i.e. in the law courts. Revealed morality calls historical experience to its aid. V. 9b is a plural 'preached' addition.

HEART OF A STRANGER: i.e., his experience, outlook, conditions.

SEVENTH YEARS AND SEVENTH DAYS

23.10-13

Every seventh year land, vineyards and olive groves must lie fallow, i.e., uncultivated. Israel's poor may gather what grows of its own accord and what they leave may be left for wild beasts. Sabbath days must be kept so as to enable beasts and men to rest. Both laws are humanitarian in purpose. Sabbath days are simultaneous, over all the land, and so presumably were seventh years, but it is difficult to think that the entire countryside remained uncultivated at the same time for a whole year. In Lev. 25 the purpose of the seventh year is to give rest to the land, and some commentators have thought that the original idea behind seventh years and seventh days is religious in the sense of a return to the original and divine order and ownership of the land. Creation then returns to its rest (Gen. 2.1-4), every seventh day of the year, and every seventh year. LET IT REST AND LIE FALLOW: Heb. 'let it drop and leave it', i.e. the land and not its produce.

12. Six days This passage confirms the original idea of the sabbath as a day of no work. SON OF YOUR BONDMAID: home-born slave. He and the resident ALIEN represent the two classes who could most easily be exploited. V. 13 is a concluding ex-hortation to obedience and against idolatry. The sentence, except for the last clause, is plural and belongs at the end of some collection of laws. Some would put it after 20.26; others after 23.19.

MAKE NO MENTION: Heb. 'do not cause to remember'. Names of idols are not to be mentioned in worship or otherwise.

THREE ANCIENT FESTIVALS

23.14-17

This festal calendar provides for three pilgrimages by the men of Israel, not empty-handed, to the local sanctuaries. The three feasts have their old agricultural and pre-Israelite names. THE FEAST OF UNLEAVENED BREAD, which marks the beginning of the barley harvest, lasts for seven days. THE FEAST OF HARVEST marks the completion of the wheat harvest in June, and is marked by the offering of first fruits. Elsewhere this feast is

styled the Feast of Weeks. THE FEAST OF INGATHERING which
marks the grape and olive harvest is also the Feast of Booths
or Tabernacles, and the autumn New Year feast.

The feasts are purely agricultural, but the process of relating
the feasts to Israel's history has begun for only one of the
feasts, i.e. UNLEAVENED BREAD. It is remarkable both that there
is no mention of Passover (unless UNLEAVENED BREAD was the
northern name for Passover and Unleavened Bread), and that
the deliverance from Egypt is linked with unleavened bread.
Yet these feasts have been admitted into Yahwism, for they
are to be celebrated TO ME; AS I COMMMANDED YOU; BEFORE
ME; BEFORE THE LORD GOD.

17. appear before The Heb. is 'see my face'. The expression
may be pre-Israelite, a reference to the faces of images of the
Canaanite gods; but more probably the reference is to Israelite
sanctuaries, e.g. to the ark. In the Heb. text the verb was
turned into the passive, 'be seen' (EVV APPEAR) to avoid the
anthropomorphism.

FOUR FINAL LAWS
23.18-19

With these laws cp. 34.25-26. **Leavened bread** and sacrificial
blood are not to be offered together, lest the leavened, fer-
mented bread contaminate the blood. Secondly the fat of the
sacrificed animals is to be burnt on the feast day itself, so as
to avoid the loss of holiness by keeping it. The third of these
laws recognized God's claim to all grown and thus earned
property. THE FIRST OF THE FIRST FRUITS, not necessarily the
earliest but certainly the best, are to be brought to the sanctuary,
i.e. presented (cp. Deut. 26.2-4). Fourthly, a kid was not to be
boiled in its mother's milk, a prohibition now explained by
reference to a Ugaritic text, *Birth of the Gods* 1.14. There at

sacrifices a kid was cooked in milk and the fields were then sprinkled with the dish to ensure their fertility. The Israelite law prohibits Canaanite magical processes in the name of Yahwism.

EPILOGUE

23.20-33 E

This passage is an epilogue, but not to the preceeding laws which are not mentioned. The commentators generally and rightly suggest that it is an epilogue to the sojourn at Sinai, or else a prologue to the journey towards, and into, Canaan. The passage is reminiscent of Deuteronomy and includes promises of a guide for Israel on the journey; of provisions, healing and long life; defeat of Israel's enemies, and gradual possession of the land of Canaan. But these promises are conditional upon Israel's obedience to the guide, the avoidance of idolatry and of fellowship with the Canaanites or their gods (cp. Deut. 28 and Lev. 26 for similar passages). The passage is in the singular except for YOUR TRANSGRESSION in v. 21, the first clause of v. 25, and YOUR HAND in v. 31.

Behold I send an angel One whose duty it is to guard and guide Israel on the way to Canaan, who has the right of forgiveness, and who bears the Lord's name. Of the desert guides which led Israel, the pillar of cloud (Ex. 13.21), the ark (Num. 10.33-36), and perhaps Hobab (Num. 10.31), the present description best fits the ark, which was a guide, bore the Name and was mighty in war (cp. 32.34; 33.14). ALL THAT I SAY, i.e., through the angel.

24. pillars Standing stones, monoliths, a regular feature of the Canaanite shrine.

25. and I will bless RSV follows Greek and Vulgate. Heb. has 'he'. Fidelity brings its blessings.

TAKE SICKNESS AWAY: cp. 15.26. I WILL FULFIL . . .—their lives will not be cut short prematurely.

27-30. Not only an angel, but the Lord's TERROR, and HORNETS will go before Israel into the land. The TERROR is a feature of 'the Holy War of the Lord' which creates a numinous panic in the hearts of all the Lord's enemies (cp. Josh. 10.10; I Sam. 7.10 etc.). The hornet could be a figure of human intervention, e.g. the Egyptians, but more likely refers to a plague. The conquest of the land will be a divinely planned military operation, by which Israel will gradually take over the land, LITTLE BY LITTLE, as they increase in numbers. This will prevent a conquered but unoccupied land from becoming uncultivated and the haunts of wild beasts. The verse also indicates the difficulty of the terrain, which could be conquered only in piecemeal fashion at this early date.

31-33. This promised programme then leads on to three further promises or commands: (*a*) Israel's occupation may be only gradual, but her eventual boundaries will comprise the area between four points: FROM THE RED SEA, i.e. Sea of Reeds, to the Mediterranean, and FROM THE WILDERNESS TO THE EUPHRATES (Heb. 'the river', which in OT means Euphrates). This is said to have been almost achieved in the days of Solomon (I Kings 4.21), though the limits mentioned here were never fully achieved. The OT preserves several descriptions of the territory comprised in the Promised Land, and these texts (e.g. Gen. 13.14-18; 15.18; Deut. 11.24; Isa. 27.12f.) are doubtless factors in international politics in the modern world. (*b*) The present inhabitants of the land will be driven out, however long it takes. (*c*) Until the present inhabitants are driven out, Israel must have no truck with them. Covenant with them will mean covenant with their gods, and that is idolatry. Idolatry is a SNARE which means death.

THE COVENANT AT SINAI

24.1-18

The theophany of ch. 19, the laws of chs. 20-23, lead to the ratification of the covenant in two ceremonies.

(a) God, through Moses, with the help of young men concludes a covenant with all Israel at the foot of Sinai employing a distinctive blood ritual to the accompaniment of spoken conditions (24.3-8 E).

(b) An Israelite deputation consisting of four leaders and seventy elders ascend the mount, are given a vision of the God of Israel, and partake of a meal (24.1-2, 9-11 J). This is the only vision in the Old Testament which is completely silent, i.e. is not also an audition.

The relation of these two ceremonies to each other, whether they are two accounts of the same main event, or successive ceremonies, or two originally independent ceremonies, one of which had little to do with the covenant at Sinai, cannot at present be ascertained. The Kenite origin of the J verses cannot be excluded.

THE SILENT VISION

24.1-2, 9-11 J

1-2. And he said to Moses In 20.21 (E) God spoke to the people; now he singles out Moses, giving to him still on the mountain the instructions whereby the Israelite deputation is later to ascend the mountain. The relationship with 19.20-25 (J) is not clear.

NADAB AND ABIHU: according to 28.1 they are Aaron's eldest sons who managed to remain in the Exodus tradition in spite of their wickedness (Lev. 10.1-10). AFAR OFF. Three positions

192

of worship, of graduated approach, occur:—the people who do
NOT COME UP, i.e., they are at the foot; the others, Aaron, his
sons and the seventy elders, are on the mount but not at the
summit; Moses alone is to COME NEAR. In the sequel, Ex.
24.9-11, the people are not present, and Moses is not mentioned separately. Vv. 9-11, sequel of vv. 1-2, are some of the
most astonishing and inexplicable verses of the Old Testament. The deputation ascends the mountain, and looking up-
wards into the sky they see the God of Israel, at least so far
as his feet. They do not dare to look higher, and perhaps they
could not, for under God's feet was the clear blue sky like a
blue pavement. God's only role is to be seen. He allows them
to come near but does not attempt to harm them. Their only
role is to see and behold. Nobody says anything. Then the
deputation has a meal either on the mountain or, less likely,
after they have descended. Commentators claim that the meal
is the ratification of the covenant, but of this the text says
nothing. The two fundamental activities of worship and of
everyday life—eating and drinking—are here associated. We
cannot be sure that it was a sacrificial meal, let alone a covenant meal while God looked on. CHIEF MEN: lit. 'corners'—
men who supported the community.

THE COVENANT WITH ISRAEL

24.3-8 E

Moses now relates the orally given laws to the people, who
accept ALL THE WORDS WHICH THE LORD HAS SPOKEN. ALL THE
ORDINANCES: many commentators suggest that the editor who
inserted the Book of the Covenant (20.22-23.33) into its present
place interpolated these words in this verse to make the connection. When the people give their acceptance, Moses records
in writing the terms of the covenant, and, early next day, erects

at the foot of the mountain an altar and twelve pillars, one for each tribe. Young men prepare and offer the sacrifices and presumably handle the blood. Moses divides the blood and throws half on the altar, and then reads the Book of the Covenant, i.e. he brings God into relationship with this half of the blood. Then the people orally accept the covenant in the same words as in 24.3, with the extra clause AND WE WILL BE OBEDIENT. Then the other half of the blood is thrown over the people, and described as the blood of the covenant which the Lord has just made.

Just as in some forms of covenant-making the symbols of God's presence pass between the divided animals (cp. Abraham's vision, Gen. 15.17), so Moses' reading of the law and the promise of the people take place between the two halves of the blood ritual. The divine offer and the people's acceptance take place together in a space of time and experience bounded at each end by sacrificial blood and life. Within that span is the union of will and purpose, decided upon and achieved in the covenant. Even more conclusively the divine offer and the people's acceptance are not merely contained within that span, they are covered and embraced by a third factor common to both—the blood covering the altar and the people (though not the twelve pillars). Both partners, divine and human, are joined and united so far as the matter in hand is concerned— the giving and accepting of the words of the Lord—in the blood of the animals which have been slaughtered. Whereas in the giving and accepting of the law the Lord and the people stand over against each other as contracting partners, in the blood ritual they are organically related and become united. This is the sacramental at-one-ment of the covenant relationship.

Thus, following the theophany and the oral revelation of the law, the third great act at Sinai, the covenant, is accomplished. On the basis of the spoken law now set down in writing, and further identified, not as the Decalogue yet to be written (24.

12), but as the Book of the Covenant (24.7), the covenant is concluded. Possibly vv. 4a and 7 are additions.

The covenant at Sinai really inaugurates the history of the covenant community in Israel. Covenant, as such, is the vehicle of God's kingship, the seal of his election and the form of the people of God. The content of the covenant is peace, and in turn this covenant peace is the blessing of God at rest at its goal mingled with the obedience of men accepted by God. This amalgam of blessing and obedience is the at-one-ment— the fellowship of covenant. Peace is blessing at rest in covenant, as it is also obedience fulfilled in relationship.

The covenant at Sinai is resumed at Shechem (Josh. 24), where Joshua is the mediator as was Moses at Sinai. In the Davidic covenant (II Sam. 7.8-16), the bilateral covenant receives an essential modification—it becomes tripartite. From now on the covenant between God and his people must always find room for the figure of David, or the suffering servant, or the son of man, or the Messiah. A personal third party is from now on inevitable.

The new covenant of Jeremiah apparently follows the old pattern of Sinai, but this is not so, because blood is omitted, and because Jeremiah has transferred the covenant from the tables of stone to the heart. He has thus continued the process whereby the covenant becomes personal and inward. Jesus crowns the covenant institution by bringing back the blood element—his own blood, and by personifying the covenant— 'in my blood'. Jesus becomes and is the covenant. The covenant is thus fully and actually personal and at-one-ing. This organic character of the covenant safeguards it against merely federal and legal interpretations. Covenant is the form of community, but in Christ the covenant of the community is also personal and as such universal.

At Sinai where Israel was really born, in Jeremiah where the new Israel was envisaged, and at the Last Supper where the new Israel, the Church, was launched, covenant is given

or envisaged. Covenant is the moment, the manner and the
identity of what is born, and is thus the most ancient, most
characteristic and decisive mark of the people of God. If
covenant and community are thus synonomous, in Christ they
are identical.

MOSES ON THE MOUNT

24.12-18

Vv. 12-15a are E, forming both the sequel of vv. 3-8 and the
prelude to chs. 32-34; vv. 15b-18 (P) are the introduction to
the long P section in chs. 25-31.

12. the tables of stone   So E, but J and Deuteronomy 'the two
tables of stone' (Ex. 34.1ff.; Deut. 4.13 etc.), and P 'the two
tables of the testimony'. WITH THE LAW AND THE COMMAND-
MENT are probably an addition (Deuteronomic), and WHICH
I HAVE WRITTEN should follow after and refer to the tables of
stone. THE LAW AND THE COMMANDMENT have been variously
explained, beginning with Deut. 5.31, and going on finally to
the several parts of the Talmud.

13. Joshua   Moses takes Joshua his servant, (cp. 17.9), and
presumably they both ascend the mountain, but Joshua remains
on the lower slopes (32.17). Moses' ascent is mentioned in v.
13b before he gives his instructions in v. 14, and before he
ascends in 15. AARON AND HUR are put in charge of the people
and their disputes during the absence of Moses and his lieuten-
ant. This again suggests that the arrangements said to have
been made at 18.13-27 are still in the future.

15b-18. These P verses continue 19.1-2a.

the cloud . . . the glory   Just as a royal flag is unfurled above the place where the sovereign happens to be, so the cloud covers Sinai to show that God is in residence for the time being on this mountain. The cloud is the covering of the glory which is the outward manifestation of God's presence, and in and through the cloud could be seen blazing flames of fire. SETTLED: RV 'abode'. Heb. *shakan*—'to tabernacle, dwell among'. This word is characteristic of P and expresses an important aspect of his theology. A Greek form of this word is used in John 1.14, 'dwell among us'. SEVENTH DAY: Moses draws near to God gradually. After six days Moses enters the cloud.

18. forty days Cp. the parallel in 34.28 (J). In 32.1 E says Moses was a long time on the mount, and in Deut. 9.9 this is again forty days. There was thus one period of forty days, but in Deut. 9.18 and 10.10 this one period has been duplicated. Into this one period falls the story of the golden calf. The forty days in P are the days of theophany and lawgiving (Ex. 25-31). P tells of no covenant at Sinai since, for him, all that happened at Sinai had already been contained within the covenant with the patriarchs.

THE TABERNACLE AND ITS MINISTRY:
THE PRIESTLY LAWS

25.1-40

The Priestly writer preserves the divine instructions of a fairly precise specification for the construction of the Tabernacle, a curtained tent, a portable temple or sanctuary, and also for the dress and consecration of a ministry for this shrine. Ch. 25 prescribes for the ark, a table for bread and a candlestick; ch. 26 for the curtains on their wooden frame; ch. 27 for the courtyard of the shrine with its altar of burnt-offering; chs. 28 and 29 for the attendant ministry, and the daily sacrifice. 29.43-46 is a section of great importance explaining the purpose and meaning of this shrine in terms of Israel's deliverance from Egypt. Chs. 30 and 31 prescribe for another altar (incense); for the financial support of the shrine; for a washing bowl; oil; incense; the foremen for the work and for the observance of the sabbath.

The instructions given in chs. 25-31 are said to be carried out in chs. 35-40 (29.1-39 is repeated in Lev. 8), They reappear in the same words, with the verbs changed from future into past, and with certain other alterations. Thus the plans are carried out and the Tabernacle is made and begins to function.

In Ex. 33.7-12 (E.) we are told that it was Moses' custom to pitch a tent outside the camp. What is the connection between the Tabernacle of chs. 25-31 and the tent of 33.7-12? In theory of course they are the same tent, and it may be assumed that a shrine-tent existed and was used by Moses and his people in the wilderness. Nevertheless in size, function and significance the two tents are very different.

Moses' tent was a simple nomad tent, but it has been estimated that the Tabernacle required $1\frac{1}{4}$ tons of gold, $4\frac{1}{4}$ tons of silver, 3 tons of bronze, not to mention the jewels, the wood and other materials.

Moses could himself pitch the tent of 33.7-12; but the erection of the Tabernacle was a far bigger task; Joshua is the guardian of the tent (33.11); but 8580 Levites guarded the Tabernacle (Num. 4.48). The tent is outside the camp (Ex. 33.7) but the Tabernacle at the camp centre (Num. 2). The tent is mainly for purposes of revelation (33.7-11), whereas the Tabernacle is not only the centre of a complex sacrificial system but expresses a theology of the Presence of God, of God's dwelling with the people in such a way as to relate his transcendence to his manifestation among them.

The Priestly Tabernacle: Its Existence

The Tabernacle in its size, costly materials, ministry and significance is the transfiguration of the simple tent pitched and used by Moses. In the main three explanations of the elaboration are possible.

(a) The Tabernacle and the tent are one and the same, and the more elaborate description must supplement the simpler account. The commentaries show how difficult in practical terms this solution is.

(b) The modern reconstruction from the days of Wellhausen has denied that this Tabernacle ever existed. It is an ideal reconstruction emanating from the priests of Jerusalem in pre-exilic and post-exilic days after the destruction of Solomon's temple. Moses' tent was the origin and Solomon's temple the model for this purely fictional and imaginary Tabernacle. But though many of the directions for the making of the Tabernacle and its component parts lack precision, nevertheless, Ex. 35-40 are a record of work done, of things made and assembled, a Tabernacle constructed and completed. The only safe conclusion from these chapters is that this Tabernacle was made and once did exist.

(c) If the priestly Tabernacle with all its elaboration is not
a desert institution, and if it is not, in view of all its actuality,
a fiction of priestly imagination, then it must be fitted in somewhere else. P says the Tabernacle was set up at Shiloh (Josh.
18.1; 19.51 and cp. I Sam. 2.22b [not in LXX]), and the
Chronicler places it at Gibeon (II Chron. 1.3-6a; cp. I Chron.
16.39; 21.29). Various references to the ark could of course
also refer to the Tabernacle, but for various reasons none
of these references to the Tabernacle, or to the ark alone, are
free of objection. A possible solution for the origin of the
Tabernacle may be discovered in the tent that David erected
for the ark at Jerusalem (II Sam. 6.17 and cp. I Kings 1.39;
2.28). By the days of David, the costly materials, the elaborate
design, the skilled labour and the advanced theology of the
Tabernacle, not to mention its necessity as the home of the
ark, are all present. P's Tabernacle may then have been
David's tent and so the model for Solomon's Temple. (See M.
Haran, 'The Complex of Ritual Acts Performed Inside the
Tabernacle' in *Scripta Hierosolymitana*, Vol. VIII: *Studies
in the Bible* ed. Chaim Rabin, Jerusalem, 1961, pp. 272-302.)

THE GIFT OF MATERIALS FOR THE SANCTUARY

25.1-9

The LORD said to Moses   The Lord instructs Moses, who by
24.18 is on the mountain top and in the cloud, to ask for an
OFFERING: lit. a heave offering, a portion separated from a
larger amount and then offered as a contribution. The contribution, though required, must also be voluntary from ready
hearts, and would consist of metals, fabrics, hair and skins,
wood, oil, spices and precious stones. The fabrics are for the
curtains of the Sanctuary, the hair and skins for coverings
over the curtains. The raw materials and the construction are

the people's offering, but the pattern and the use of the structure are divinely conferred. THAT I MAY DWELL IN THEIR MIDST offers the barest statement of Israel's faith in the Tabernacling Presence, the constituting principle of the people of God. BLUE: better purple-blue or violet; PURPLE: better purple-red; they are probably Phenician dyes, as FINE TWINED LINEN is probably Egyptian. GOATSKINS is uncertain but either some kind of dolphin or sea cow or treated leather imported possibly from Egypt is meant. EPHOD: cp. 28.6. SANCTUARY: lit. a holy place. TABERNACLE: lit. a dwelling. The Heb. root for 'dwell' in v. 8 is the same as for Tabernacle in v. 9 and is the word from which *Shekinah*, the post-biblical term for the Presence or appearance of God, is derived.

TABERNACLE is used in two senses by P: (*a*) of the entire fabric of the sanctuary and (*b*) the tapestry curtains on the frames of the dwelling itself. Besides SANCTUARY and TABERNACLE other descriptions are Dwelling of Testimony; Tent of Testimony; Tent; and most frequently Tent of Meeting.

8. I show you The model of the sanctuary as with other ancient Near Eastern temples, is a revelation from God. This idea of a heavenly prototype is expressly applied in 25.40 to the ark, table and lampstand, in 26.30 to the Tabernacle, and in 27.8 to the altar, and some have claimed that these were the original nucleus of the priestly narrative. Others have claimed that a distinction must be made between an original and simple tent structure—a portable red leather tent such as was used by Arabs with its accompanying Ark or box—and a later elaboration derived from Canaanite ideas and illustrated in the structure of frames (26.15-50), reminiscent of the trellised throne room of El in the Ras Shamra documents, in the division of outer and inner parts of the sanctuary as in the Solomonic and other temples, and in the Phenician-like furnishings.

THE ARK

25.10-22 (37.1-9)

(Consult the Commentary on 33.5 and cp. Deut. 10.1-5.)

The first thing that must be made is the ark, the central,
focal point, the single most sacred and significant feature of
the sanctuary. It is a portable box of acacia wood about
3¾ by 2¼ by 2¼ feet, plated within and without with gold, the
top of each side edged with a rim or moulding of gold, and
surmounted with a cover or lid of gold—the mercy seat—
but separate from the box. In turn the golden lid was
decorated with two golden cherubim—one at each end—
soldered to the lid, but with wings overarching the lid. Between the wings and the lid is the centre of the invisible
Presence, whence God meets and speaks with Moses, and
within the box the two stone tables of the Decalogue.

AN ARK: not the same Heb. word as Noah's ark, which was
a ship; nor Moses' ark which was a cradle. It has several
names in the Old Testament like ark of the Lord; ark of the
covenant of the Lord (Deut); ark of the testimony, (P), besides
several synonyms like 'strength', 'name', 'glory' etc. A CUBIT
is about eighteen inches. PURE GOLD: more refined than
ordinary gold. Pure gold was used for the ark, its lid, for the
bread table and its vessels; for the candlestick and its utensils,
for the incense altar and for parts of the High Priest's dress;
ordinary gold for the less sacred parts (see Driver's Commentary on 25.3). MOULDING: either a rim, on which the lid
rested, or into which it fitted, or a golden wreath around the
four sides of the box. Four RINGS of ordinary gold fixed probably to the short sides were to be permanently fitted with poles
of acacia wood plated with ordinary gold for transport.
THE TESTIMONY: lit. the attestation or affirmation—P's name
for the Decalogue. For P the ark is at least a container. A
MERCY SEAT: the word means either a lid or cover, or a

propitiatory—a means of propitiation—and symbolically also
the footstool of the divine Presence.

18. two cherubim Probably winged sphinxes—winged lions
with human heads. In Solomon's temple the cherubim are part
of the Holy of Holies, and are in the sanctuary, for the ark
is carried in and placed underneath the wings of the cherubim.
Here in Ex. P attaches the cherubim to the lid of the ark,
and their wings overshadow the mercy seat. Images of tutelary
deities are customary at the entrance of temples and palaces
in the Fertile Crescent, and the cherubim were doubtless
attendant on the Lord, as overshadowing, adoring and inter-
ceding.

22. There I will meet with you Two functions of the tent of
Meeting (33.7-11), namely, meeting with God, and revelation
from God, are here transferred to the ark, and to a particular
part of it—THERE, i.e. above the lid and between the cherubim.
The ark thus appears in a fourfold function—the container
of the law; the bearer and propitiatory of the Presence; the
point of contact for God and Moses, and the place of origin
of divine revelation. The military, guiding and processional
functions of the ark are of course not mentioned in the
present context.

In 36.8ff. the Tabernacle is made before the ark, and in P
both Tabernacle and ark are made without reference to the
golden calf episode. In Deut. 10 the construction of the ark is
one of the sequels of that episode (Deut. 9.13-21 and cp. Ex.
33.5).

THE TABLE

25.23-30 (**37**.10-16)

A table of acacia wood (LXX: of gold), 3 by 1½ by 2¼ feet,

was overlaid with pure gold and with a golden moulding. It
also had a frame with a gold moulding. The moulding on the
edge of the table may have been the same as the moulding
on the frame, but if the frame was some way down the table
legs, then there were two mouldings. The rings were attached
to the frame and so the moving parts (rings and poles) were
some distance from the table surface. The table carried plates
and dishes for incense, and flagons and bowls for wine liba-
tions, all of fine gold. The real purpose of the table was to
bear the BREAD OF THE PRESENCE, lit. 'bread of the Face'—holy
bread (I Sam. 21.4f.), continual bread (Num. 4.7), bread in
two rows (Lev. 24.6). Exodus does not give any hint that the
bread was food for the Lord, but it was an offering to him,
marking his Presence and acknowledging him as the Lord of
sustenance. The Old Testament nowhere else mentions the
use of wine in connection with the Presence bread.

THE LAMPSTAND

25.31-40 (37.17-24)

The one-piece trident-shaped lampstand consisted of a base
and central upright stem from which on each side three
branches went out and up. At the ends of the stem and the
branches were lamps (v. 37). ITS CUPS were modelled on the
stem and petals of almond blossoms and were for decoration.
The position of the four cups in the main stem is uncertain,
but three appear to have come at intervals on each of the
lateral arms. SNUFFERS are either tongs (Isa. 6.6), or tweezers
for adjusting the wick. TO GIVE LIGHT: the purpose is utili-
tarian, but because of the association of the lampstand with
the ark and the table in this chapter, and in the summary of
40, the lampstand marked the Presence of the Lord. 27.21 and
30.8 suggest that the lamps were lit each night. There was a

light at Shiloh (I Sam. 3.3); there were ten lampstands in Solomon's temple. W. F. Albright has found at Tell Beit Mersim terra cotta lamps dating from not later than 900 BC with places for seven wicks. The Arch of Titus at Rome portrays a table and lampstand among the articles taken from Herod's temple.

THE TABERNACLE

26.1-37 (36.8-38)

This chapter deals with the Tabernacle made of curtains, 26.1-14, then with the gold plated wooden frames, over and around which the curtains are to hang (vv. 15-30), and lastly with a richly decorated veil (vv. 31-37).

THE CURTAINS

26.1-14

The TABERNACLE, or Dwelling, is simply the CURTAINS in position. Ten curtains, each 28 by 4 cubits (42 by 6 feet), of superior fine linen with violet blue, purple and scarlet tapestry decorated with cherubim are to be joined together to make two curtains which are then to be joined by one hundred blue loops and fifty golden clasps to form one single curtain 40 by 28 cubits (60 by 42 feet). For travelling purposes the two curtains could be unhooked, but in use they were spread over the framework (15-30), so as to show the decoration inwards. The looped edges of both curtains formed a central seam, and this was placed over the veil which divided the two parts of the dwelling. Also the length of the single curtain was 28 cubits, and this length really became the breadth when the two curtains were joined to make a length of 40 cubits. These 28 cubits then covered two sides, each 10 cubits, and a ceiling of 10 cubits, in all 30 cubits, and so the curtain of 28 cubits failed to reach the ground on each side by one cubit. This cubit was the height of the base into which the frames of the structure fitted.

7. Curtains of goats' hair These serve as a first covering or

tent over the curtains which form the Tabernacle. Eleven curtains each 30 by 4 cubits (45 by 6 feet) make a curtain 30
by 44 cubits (45 by 66 feet), the two parts, one of five
curtains and the second of six, being joined by one hundred
loops and FIFTY bronze clasps. THE SIXTH CURTAIN in the
second piece hung double as a sort of valance over the front
side of the dwelling. This first covering is two cubits longer
than the Tabernacle curtain and therefore reaches to the
ground at the back and sides, so covering the Tabernacle
curtain and the bases of the framework over which the Tabernacle curtain did not extend. On this view the reference in v.
12 to a half curtain left over must be a gloss, because all the
curtain available, i.e. 2 cubits doubled in front, 30 along the
side and 10 at the back make up the 44 cubits of the curtain.
But the curtain may have been made with this much 'spare'
to provide for tucking, shrinking etc. The first covering or
tent was then itself covered by two further coverings, one of
rams' skins dyed red, and the other of GOATSKINS, better
dugong skins. The Hebrew text mentions two coverings but
RSV speaks of one COVERING only.

THE WOODEN FRAME OF THE TABERNACLE

26.15-30

26.1-14 have depicted an elaborate nomad tent with four
coverings but without any supports. The supports are now
supplied in the form of the wooden frame about to be described. The two parts, tent and frame, are necessary to each
other, and make impossible any suggestion that the tent
and frame are derived from different literary traditions.
Recognizing the nomadic origin of the tent, we do not need to
postulate Solomon's temple as the origin of the framework.
The tent needed an elaborate framework, and these dimen-

sions became the prototype for the dimensions of Solomon's
temple.

UPRIGHT FRAMES 10 by 1½ cubits (15 by 2¼ feet) are the
framework of the two long sides and back of the dwelling.
The translation FRAMES is adopted by RSV from Kennedy,
and is an inspired guess to replace the old translation 'beams'
or 'boards'. Each frame has TWO TENONS, lit. hands, i.e. uprights joined by cross pieces at the top, middle and bottom.
The frame had two extensions downwards which fitted into
slots in silver pedestals. FOR FITTING TOGETHER: Heb. 'joined
a woman to her sister'. This can hardly mean that the frames
went in pairs, but probably that each frame had two uprights
which matched and were joined. There were twenty frames
on each of the south (lit. negeb) and north sides and six on
the west (lit. sea) side. The six frames forming the end would
be nine cubits wide, and this would leave one cubit for the
thickness of the frames at each side. So the frames were nine
inches thick.

24. The details here are difficult. At each corner of the west
end, that is, the rear, two extra frames are somehow to be
fitted, making a total of eight frames at this end. They are
corner supports or buttresses, so that the end frame on
each side of the west or rear end was double or twinned.
SEPARATE BENEATH BUT JOINED AT THE TOP presupposes two
frames at an angle, but then the sockets would have to be an
angle.

26. Fifteen horizontal BARS are to be placed on the two long
sides and the rear end. A middle bar is to run the whole length
of each of the three sides—so two bars would be 45 feet long.
Above and below this one-piece bar were two more bars
along part of the side. The bars plated with gold pass through
golden rings attached to the gold plated frames.

THE VEIL AND THE SCREEN

26.31-37

A veil of the same material as the curtain of the dwelling is to hang from hooks on four gold plated pillars of acacia wood fixed in silver bases, so as to divide the dwelling in two parts, the rear portion—the holy of holies—a cube of 10 cubits (15 feet), and the front portion 20 by 10 cubits (30 by 15 feet). Solomon's temple was 60 by 20 cubits. The ark with its MERCY SEAT is to be put behind the veil within the cube, but the table and the lampstand this side of the veil, in the holy place, on the north and south sides respectively.

A screen of embroidered linen without cherubim is to hang at the front entrance—THE DOOR OF THE TENT, four golden rings attached to gold plated wooden pillars standing in bronze sockets. The simpler curtain and the bronze sockets mark the distance from the supreme holiness.

THE ALTAR AND THE COURT

27.1-21 (38.1-20)

THE ALTAR

27.1-8

27.20-21 have no parallel in ch. 38.

Moses is commanded to make an acacia wood altar overlaid with bronze, 5 by 5 by 3 cubits high ($7\frac{1}{2}$ by $7\frac{1}{2}$ by $4\frac{1}{2}$ feet). Cp. for these dimensions II Chron. 6.13.

1. the altar There was one altar, the altar of burnt offering (30.28), the bronze altar (38.30). The word for altar means literally the place where you slay. Since the altar is presumably empty and without a top, it would be filled with stones or earth on which the fire would be lit. Otherwise the wooden interior would be destroyed. At each corner of the altar are HORNS, bronze plated projections big enough to hold. To these horns blood was applied (cp. Ex. 29.12; Lev. 4.18; 16.18); and to touch them meant sanctuary for any person (I Kings 1.50 etc.). The altar is serviced by a variety of bronze tools, pots and shovels to remove ITS ASHES (lit. fat) i.e. to catch the fat of sacrifice, and BASINS for holding and throwing sacrificial blood.

4. a grating Half way down the altar is a ledge; from this ledge to the base is a bronze grating or grille which supports the ledge and also receives the blood. The altar is portable by means of bronze plated poles inserted through bronze plated rings attached to the top edge of the grating. The PEGS may be tent pegs but their use is not mentioned.

THE COURT

27.9-19

The court is a rectangle lying east and west 100 by 50 cubits (150 by 75 feet) enclosed by white linen hangings 5 cubits (7½ feet) high. The entrance was at the centre of the east front and was protected by an embroidered screen. Twenty pillars on the north and south sides, ten on the west, support the hangings from silver hooks. The silver FILLETS may be rods between the pillars or silver bands on the pillars, but their purpose is really unknown. The pillars stand in bronze bases. The diagram in Kennedy's article on the Tabernacle in Hasting's *Dictionary of the Bible* (Vol. IV, 1902, p. 657), shows that either one pillar is missing from the specification or else the entrance to the court is not central. Did they 'cut a corner' and so obviate the necessity of another pillar?

The EAST side has an interesting arrangement. It is divided into three parts—the central 20 cubits (30 feet) consists of a screen similar to that at the entrance to the dwelling, hung from four pillars. On each side are 15 cubit (22½ feet) hangings from three pillars.

The plan of the court exhibits the designer's love of symmetry. From the above mentioned diagram it is clear that if the court be regarded as consisting of two squares 50 by 50 cubits, the ark will occupy the central place in the one square as the altar does in the other square. The altar is the bond between the dwelling and the front entrance as well as the place for sacrifice and sanctuary.

LAMP OIL

27.20-21

Cp. Lev. 24.2-3. These verses, which presuppose the consecration of Aaron and his sons, provide for gifts of oil from the

people for a sanctuary light set up in front of the veil of the most
Holy Place.

continually   Not continuously, but regularly; the lamps were
to be trimmed and lit each night. The Heb. word *tamid* figures
prominently, for instance in connection with the breastpiece
(28.29), diadem (28.38) and incense (30.8). STATUTE FOR EVER:
The Heb. word may mean 'regulation' or 'presented portion'.
The law for the lamp leads naturally to the arrangements for
the priests. AND HIS SONS: The sharing of these duties with
the sons of Aaron is mentioned only here. In the parallel
passage in Lev. 24.1-4 Aaron alone serves, and no mention is
made of his sons. Many scholars think that AND HIS SONS
have been erroneously inserted in Exodus.

THE PRIESTLY GARMENTS

28.1-43 (39.1-31)

INTRODUCTION

28.1-5

Moses the supreme and unique personality in Israel is to
prepare priestly garments for Aaron and his four sons in
readiness for their consecration to the priestly office. Aaron
and his garments are the real subject of this chapter because
he typifies the office, dress and function of the Zadokite High
Priest.

1. to serve me as priests Lit. to be a priest to (or for) me.
The priests were caretakers at sanctuaries, offerers of sacrifices, guardians of Urim and Tummim, givers of oracles,
legislators of *toroth* (laws), archivists, teachers and ministers,
and dispensers of blessings. ME or MY (Heb. 'to me'), three
times in vv. 1, 3, 4, emphasizes the theocentric axis of their
functions. NADAB AND ABIHU: these two (cp. 24.1, 9 and Lev.
10.1-3) died in the unlawful execution of their office. The
third son, Eleazar, succeeded Aaron and was eventually regarded as the Aaronic ancestor of the Zadokite priesthood.
Moses outlived Aaron and actually inducted Eleazar into his
father's office (Num. 20.28; Deut. 10.6). Ithamar, Aaron's
fourth son, was apparently the ancestor of the priest Eli at
Shiloh.

2. holy garments The garments are considered holy in themselves, whereas today we should be more likely to consider
them holy because of those who wear them, or because of
the exercises performed when such garments were worn;

213

though, properly, holiness belongs only to spirit and so to the personal. ABILITY . . . ABLE MIND: the underlying Heb. words speak of wisdom.

4. garments   The number of items (six in all) and their variety suggest that probably this list illustrates various stages in the increase of priestly clothing through the centuries. The four priestly garments listed in vv. 40-43, the tunic, trousers, girdle and cap, are worn by all priests and are actual clothing; but the ROBE, EPHOD, BREASTPIECE and diadem are worn by Aaron only, and are outer additions with a religious significance. Their more splendid and costly character indicates that they are appropriate for use in the Holy Place.

5. gold   The material to be used was the same as for the curtain of the Tabernacle with the addition of gold thread— the person was then more nobly adorned than the place.

THE EPHOD

28.6-12

This was a decorated garment worn front and back above the waist, or more probably as a loin cloth below the waist (cp. II Sam. 6.14). It was probably open at both sides, the front and back being joined by SHOULDER PIECES (straps) over the shoulders, and held to the body by a BAND or girdle of the same material (v. 8). Gold chains attached to the straps held gold filigree work in position, and in turn in this work TWO ONYX STONES were set, one on each shoulder, each stone bearing the names of six Israelite tribes arranged IN THE ORDER OF THEIR BIRTH. When Aaron wore this garment, he was authorized not only to represent Israel, but in a sense to take the twelve tribes into the Presence of God, and to present his people to the Lord by way of remembrance. Samuel (I Sam.

2.18f.) and David (II Sam. 6.14) wore ephods—priestly garments of simpler form than the foregoing.

THE BREASTPIECE OF JUDGMENT

28.13-30

The Hebrew word for BREASTPIECE is obscure, but it obviously describes a pouch or flat muff, some nine inches square, worn over the ephod, attached by two gold rings at two corners by gold chains to the ephod straps. The two lower rings were at the back of the breastpiece and were tied by a LACE OF BLUE (v. 28) to two rings at the bottom ends of the ephod straps. Thus the breastpiece was kept in position flat on the body. The front of the pouch was dressed with gold settings in which were set four rows of jewels, three in a row, each jewel bearing the name of an Israelite tribe. The identity of the twelve precious stones is not always certain; with the list cp. Ezek. 28.13; Rev. 21.19-20. LXX omits Ex. 28.26-28, these verses offering a further account of how the pouch was attached.

29-30. The pouch had a double function. On its front it bore Israel's twelve names, and within it, the two stones, Urim and Tummim, were secreted. Urim (? No) and Tummim (? Yes) are the means whereby divine answers are given to the queries of worshippers who put questions to which 'yes' or 'no' could be given as an answer. These stones give the article its name, BREASTPIECE OF JUDGMENT. So the pouch is a memorial of Israel before God, and a means of revelation to Israel from God. Thus Aaron or the High Priest brings Israel's need and lot to God, and makes known God's will to his people, an Old Testament anticipation of the Apostle and High Priest of Heb. 3.1.

THE VIOLET ROBE

28.31-35

Aaron and his successors are also to wear a long, sleeveless
one-piece violet (RSV BLUE) ROBE, with a strengthened OPEN-
ING FOR THE HEAD, and with a skirt decorated with POME-
GRANATES, and in between the pomegranates a series of golden
bells. The ringing bells may serve an apotropaic purpose, but
on the other hand if they did not ring, the silence would
signify some mishap to Aaron alone within. THE ROBE OF THE
EPHOD, that is, worn under it, rather than over it, as the order
of the garments would suggest.

THE PLATE, TURBAN AND COAT

28.36-39

A PLATE or diadem of pure gold was to be fastened by a
blue lace to the front of the high priestly TURBAN, and inscribed like a signet with the words HOLY TO THE LORD. These
words mark the special consecration of the High Priest—his
'belongingness' to God. The Hebrew word for PLATE means
something shining or a flower, and some commentators have
thought of a golden flower on the turban. Aaron's wearing of
the TURBAN OF FINE LINEN with its golden attachment betokens
his double role. When wearing it Aaron will be held responsible for any ritual error or fault, but he will also be marked
out as Israel's representative before the divine Presence, and
able to effect God's acceptance of the people's offerings in
spite of any errors. Aaron is also to have a long coat like a
cassock in a check design, the already mentioned turban—a
feature of royal dress in Ezek. 21.26—and a ceremonial, embroidered, girdle. These parts of his dress, then, are meant to
elicit the grace of God, and perhaps to represent it.

This ceremonial adornment of the High Priest should now be contrasted with the simple garments he wears when he makes atonement. After making atonement, he puts off the ordinary linen garments of the priest, bathes and then resumes his garments (cp. Ex. 28.1-39 and Lev. 16.4, 23f.). He atones in humble dress and then resumes his royal-priestly dress, which was doubtless a legacy of royal regalia.

THE GARMENTS OF THE PRIESTS

28.40-43

By contrast the COATS AND GIRDLES AND CAPS with the LINEN BREECHES are described in four verses. V. 41 anticipates 29.1, 5-9, and may be a later addition, for in v. 41 both Aaron and his sons are anointed with oil, but in 29.7 Aaron only. ORDAIN THEM represents the Heb. technical term 'fill the hand', used to describe appointment to priestly office.

THE CONSECRATION OF THE PRIESTS

29.1-37 (Lev. 8)

This section describes the procedure to be followed in the
installation of Aaron and his sons into the priestly office,
though the installation is actually performed in Lev. 8. Indeed the terminology and usages of several parts of Ex. 29
presuppose Lev. 1-7, so that it appears Lev. 1-7 must have
been in operation when Ex. 29 was written.

1-9. Moses must bring to the door of the tent of meeting a
bullock and two rams, and, in a basket, unleavened bread,
cakes mixed with oil, and wafers of fine wheat flour anointed
with oil, and then summon Aaron and his sons. Moses must
next WASH THEM and robe Aaron (the item called a PLATE in
28.36 is here, in v. 6, called a CROWN), and anoint him by
pouring oil upon his head, and then dress his sons. This
procedure, of which the anointing is the decisive act, accom-
plishes the installation. It is laid down by a PERPETUAL
STATUTE that the priesthood is to be hereditary. The robing of
Aaron's sons expresses this, but one wonders whether this
robing was accompanied by some form of words which expressed the perpetual statute. Otherwise not a word is said.
Perhaps the whole ceremony was to be carried on in absolute
silence, but perhaps we are to suppose that defining sentences
were uttered at intervals. Thus Moses may have named the
separate items of clothing as he put them on Aaron. Perhaps
formulae were also uttered to accompany the actions mentioned in vv. 10b, 15b and 19b. Perhaps also the defining
clauses occurring later in the chapter were spoken. Cp. 14b,
IT IS A SIN OFFERING; 18b IT IS A BURNT OFFERING TO THE
LORD; IT IS A PLEASING ODOUR, AN OFFERING BY FIRE TO THE
LORD; and cp. also vv. 22b; 25b; 28. In Lev. 8-5 Moses utters

an introductory, authorizing sentence to the congregation, and concludes the ceremonies of the first day with some instructions to Aaron and his sons (Lev. 8.31-35).

THUS YOU SHALL ORDAIN: (Heb. You shall fill the hand of) AARON AND HIS SONS (v. 9).

10-14. Priestly ordination must now be vested in sacrifice. Moses is to slay the bullock as a sin offering on behalf of Aaron and his sons, who identify the sacrifice as their own by placing THEIR HANDS upon it (cp. Lev. 4). Some of the blood is to be smeared on THE HORNS OF THE ALTAR, and the rest poured out AT THE BASE OF THE ALTAR. No part of the sin offering could be eaten by the offerers, but certain portions of the beast were to be burnt on the altar, and the rest burnt outside the camp.

15-18. Moses is to offer the first ram as a burnt offering wholly destroyed apart from the blood. This offering betokens the complete consecration of the offerers, and was designed to please God and so gain his favour.

19-34. Moses is to offer the second ram as an installation sacrifice in the form of a peace offering involving a cultic meal (vv. 31-34, cp. Lev. 3). The blood ritual is more complicated, for it is to be applied not only to the altar, which was customary, but also to parts of the persons of Aaron and his sons, and, mixed with the anointing oil, to Aaron and his sons and their garments. The blood is thus to create a partnership in holiness and function between altar, priests and their clothes. The application of blood to the persons of the priests calls for Dillmann's famous note (quoted by McNeile): 'The priest must have consecrated ears to listen at all times to God's holy voice, consecrated hands continually to do holy works, and consecrated feet always to walk in holy ways.'

22. The selected portions of THE RAM correspond, with the exception of the RIGHT THIGH, to the portions prescribed for the peace offering (Lev. 3.3-5). This portion was normally the priest's, but since there are no priests as yet, it is added to the portions to be burnt. The clause FOR IT IS A RAM OF ORDINATION (lit. 'of fillings', cp. 'fill the hand'), authorizes (verbally) the exception. These portions with one sample of each cereal offering in the basket (Ex. 29.2) are to be put in the HANDS (lit. palms) of Aaron and his sons, and then waved and offered. To WAVE is to move the gift towards and from the altar.

26. Moses is to have the waved breast of ram as his portion on this occasion, but thereafter the priests are to have the breast and the thigh as their portion. Vv. 29f. interrupt the arrangements, and prescribe that Aaron's successors must wear his garments, and in particular wear them on SEVEN successive days during their ordination. The OUTSIDER (v. 33) denotes somebody who is not a priest. Vv. 31-34 say that the cultic meal was to be eaten at the door of the tent of meeting, and anything left over was to be burnt.

35-37. The (sacrificial ?) ceremony of each day is to be repeated for seven days, and every day also a bull is to be offered as a sin offering, to preserve the sanctity of the altar. This bull is probably different from the one mentioned in 29.1, 10-14. Atonement (=At-one-ment) is here said to be effected by a peace offering. This idea is unique in Priestly law, and is not mentioned in Lev. 8. The Heb. verb for OFFER A SIN OFFERING is literally 'unsin'.

MOST HOLY: lit. 'holy of holies' to express the superlative.

SACRIFICES AND PRESENCE

29.38-46

DAILY SACRIFICES

29.38-42a

This law occurs more fully in Num. 28.3-8, and, since this section interrupts the connection between vv. 37 and 43, it is probable that it has been interpolated here from the Numbers Table of Sacrifices. As a fundamental act of worship it illustrates also a fundamental feature of the priestly office. A lamb with flour, wine and oil is to be offered each morning, and a second lamb with a cereal offering etc. in the evening. This double sacrifice reflects post-exilic usage, for, as II Kings 16.15 shows, the pre-exilic custom was a morning sacrifice, and in the evening a meal offering only. A TENTH MEASURE (of an ephah) is about $6\frac{1}{2}$ pints, and A FOURTH OF A HIN would be about $2\frac{2}{3}$ pints.

PEOPLE, PRIESTS AND PRESENCE

29.42b-46

Note the resumption of the divine first person. WHERE and THERE refer to the door of the tent of meeting where the revelation, consecration and sacrifice all take place. God meets YOU (plural), people, and speaks with YOU (sing.), Moses; God also meets Israel, and in his manifestation the tent, the altar and the priesthood will be consecrated.

43. it shall be sanctified IT originally meant the altar (v. 37),

in the present context it means THE DOOR OF THE TENT (v. 42);
but Greek and Syriac read 'I will be sanctified'. The really de-
cisive consecrating agency is the GLORY of the Presence of God.
The dwelling is thus the link between the deliverance from
Egypt and the Tabernacling Presence. Israel was BROUGHT . . .
OUT OF THE LAND OF EGYPT THAT I MIGHT DWELL AMONG THEM.
The Tabernacling Presence is the constitutive principle of the
People of God. The autokerygmatic, authenticating formula,
I AM THE LORD THEIR GOD, marks the conclusion. (This shows
that chs. 30-31 are a separate section.)

A CULTIC MISCELLANY

30.-31.18

These chapters form an appendix concerned with the altar of incense (30.1-10), the tax for worship (30.11-16), the bronze laver (30.17-21), the anointing oil (30.22-33), the incense (30.34-38), the sanctuary craftsmen (31.1-11) the sabbath (31.12-17) and the tables of stone (31.18). These passages all come from P except 31.18b, which is from E.

THE ALTAR OF INCENSE

30.1-10

Reference to this altar is strangely missing from its expected place in ch. 25 and again in 26.34 (where the Samaritan version places this passage). So these verses are either deliberately placed here, or else they are a secondary addition reflecting post-exilic custom, or possibly they represent Solomon's addition (cp. I Kings 7.48) to the cultic legacy bequeathed to him by his father, and substantially contained in Ex. 25-29. The verses describe how the altar was to be made, where it was to be placed and how it was to be used.

This ALTAR, of gold-plated acacia wood, was $1\frac{1}{2}$ feet long and broad and 3 feet high. At each top corner it had the horn projections, and also had the moulding, rings and carrying poles like the ark and table. The altar was to be placed BEFORE THE VEIL BY THE ARK, i.e. before the ark but with the curtain between. (Heb. 9.4 misunderstands this passage and puts this altar inside the veil and next to the ark.) Incense was burnt upon it morning and evening, and an annual act

H   223

of propitiation (ATONEMENT) was performed upon it (Lev. 16.15-19). What the Old Testament generally calls atonement is generally called propitiation in the New Testament. The Hebrew verb means, with man as subject, to propitiate, but, with God as subject, to forgive.

THE SANCTUARY TAX

30.11-16

Upon the basis of a CENSUS each adult is to pay a half shekel sanctuary tax. In turn the tax is to serve as an act of propitiation for the maintenance of worship, and to establish the people's standing within the Lord's gracious remembrance. The RANSOM of persons serves to counteract the evil that was thought to lie within a census (cp. II Sam. 24). The tax was half a shekel and this at pre-war values was about fifteen pence. Nehemiah had to be content with one-third (Neh. 10.32). GERAHS are units of Babylonian currency.

THE BRONZE LAVER

30.17-21

A laver for ritual washing had to be provided for the use of the priests, and was placed between the sanctuary and the sacrificial altar. Either this laver was David's arrangement which was replaced by Solomon's molten sea and the ten stands, (I Kings 7.23-29), or else it was the simple post-exilic replacement of Solomon's elaborate provision. Physical cleansing is integral to cultic approach. 'Cleanliness is next to godliness', as it was wont to be said.

THE ANOINTING OIL

30.22-33

An anointing oil is to be made of four costly, scented spices from the east mixed with olive oil in certain proportions. The oil, used for anointing, healing, restoration and, as here, for the consecration of the sanctuary furniture, and of Aaron and his sons (but contrast 29.7), was not for common use on pain of excommunication.

THE INCENSE

30.34-38

Four specified ingredients in equal proportions and seasoned with salt are to make up the incense powder, and to be used exclusively in divine worship. The addition of salt meant speedier combustion. A considerable quantity of the mixture must be understood from which daily portions were taken and then ground into powder (cp. Lev. 16.12), and then put in position in a censer on the altar ready for use. Whereas the ANOINTING OIL was HOLY (vv. 31f.), the incense, like the altar (29.37), was MOST HOLY because so 'near' to the LORD The underlying theological theme WHERE I SHALL MEET WITH YOU appears once more.

THE SANCTUARY CRAFTSMEN

31.1-11

God appoints and equips the works manager for the construction of the sanctuary, and his industrial and artistic skills are the gift of God. BEZALEL is of the tribe of Judah, but HUR,

URI, and BEZALEL are also apparently a Calebite family (cp.
I Chron. 2.19f.). Bezalel's foreman or assistant is to be
Oholiab, and other able men are also to assist. References to
ABLE MEN in the service of God are a recurring feature in the
Old Testament, and cp. also II Cor. 3.6.

Even though these names are without date or detail, nevertheless the names of the sanctuary craftsmen would be
remembered. These names help to show that the sanctuary
was built. Thus Ex. 25-31 are no post-exilic fiction. They must
describe a real sanctuary of real dimensions, materials and
with named workmen. The desert period is difficult for such a
structure, but these chapters could be related to the tent
pitched by David (I Chron. 15.1; 16.1 etc.).

10. finely worked garments The meaning of the adjective is
uncertain, and 'liturgical garments', 'garments of the service',
'prescribed garments', and 'plaited garments' are all possible
renderings.

THE SABBATH

31.12-17

This passage preserves a succinct statement of the priestly
conception of the sabbath, the seventh day of the week, our
Saturday. The observance of the day is a divine decree; it is
the divinely provided proof that God is constantly at work
hallowing his people; it is a HOLY day in itself, that is, set
apart for worship; it is a day of human rest, because also it
was modelled on a day of divine rest; it is the demonstration
of the relationship between God and Israel, and the memorial
of creation. God himself WAS REFRESHED when he kept the
day. Not to keep this day is worthy of death. If YOU MAY
KNOW in v. 13 may be translated 'that men may know', then

the sabbath has also an international significance as showing
to mankind the relationship between God and Israel. The
implication is that not even the construction of the sanctuary
cancels the sabbath duty.

THE TWO TABLES OF THE TESTIMONY

31.18

This marks the end of the long interview between God and
Moses (25.1-31.18). God gives Moses THE TWO TABLES OF THE
TESTIMONY, i.e. of the ten commandments. A further note
from E adds that tables were made OF STONE, and that they
had been inscribed by God.

NOTE: *The Religious Teaching of Chapters
25-31 and 35-40*

These P sections of the Book are so rich in religious teaching
that it is only possible here to list the main ideas. Great
emphasis is laid throughout on the fact that the laws are God's
commands and word, and these divine laws are seen to
embrace many aspects of life and work. The willingness, the
obedience, the unity and united efforts, the sacrificial giving
of the people, as God's congregation, shine through the sections. The divine revelation of the pattern of the dwelling
carries with it an implied perfection in design, symmetry and
dimensions. The Holy of Holies is a perfect cube. The workmen are divinely appointed, and their craft, technique and
abilities are the gifts of the spirit. The carrying out of the
work is emphasized in chs. 37f. Divine approval is given in
the blessing of Moses at the end (39.43).

These chapters are also dominated by a numinous sense of
graduated approach to God as illustrated by personnel, liturgical acts and the use of different metals and materials. A

sanctuary light is perpetual; intercessory significance attaches to the garments and priesthood of Aaron; remembrance figures in the two onyx stones of the ephod, in the twelve name stones of the breastpiece, and in Urim and Tummim.

Above all and to crown all is the controlling theme of the Presence of God. God meets with Israel (25.22), dwells with his people and sanctifies them with his glorious Presence, and accompanies them on their journeys. The doctrine is expressed in 29.42-46 and again in 40.34-38. If J E emphasizes the Lord as the great I AM, equally in P the Lord is the great Object and Presence, the great ME of Israel's awareness and worship.

THE CRISIS OF THE CALF AND ITS CONSEQUENCES

32.-34.35

The main analysis followed here would allocate the material to the sources thus:

J   32.25-34; 33.1-4; 33.12-34.28.
E   32.1-24, 35; 33.5-11.
P   34.29-35.

There may however, be some editorial or Deuteronomic material also present as in 32.9-14. Other commentators divide the material differently and there is little agreement. Ex. 32-34 are probably the most difficult chapters in the book. To study them in the light of the source analysis of the literary critics, or of the literary units of the form-critics, or of the cultic origin and transmission proposed by the liturgical critics, or of the even more strangely named methods applied by the so-called traditio-historical school, is to realize the chaos of scholarship into which these chapters have been thrown. A big book would be required to bring some order into the investigation. The present writer believes that the source criticism is still the best solution, provided that one principle is borne in mind. The chapters present themselves to us as containing stories of what really happened, and must always be studied with that in mind.

31.18 links Moses' sojourn on the mount with chs. 32-34. In P the sojourn is contained in chs. 25-31 (compare 24.15b-18), whereas in E it begins in 24.12-15a and is said to end in 31.18. There is nothing intrinsically improbable in Moses' long withdrawal to the mount, for it served a double purpose. On the one hand Moses had accomplished a great mission, and a considerable part of his life's work lay behind him. The withdrawal then undoubtedly served as a time for retrospective evaluation, and he examined an accomplished stretch of his life in terms of his vocation. On the other hand the completion of the covenant at Sinai marked a decisive point in his mission, and plans for the future must be prepared. Part of that plan was undoubtedly the ten commandments, and the organization of the life of the people which such commandments would imply. In the long withdrawal, then, Moses was preoccupied with the meaning of his own immediate past and with the planning for the immediate future of his companions. Against that background the events now to be related are to be understood.

THE GOLDEN CALF

32.1-6

In the absence of MOSES the people virtually make AARON their leader, and request him to make a visible God or GODS as substitute for the invisible Lord. Aaron agrees, and, out of the golden earrings of the people which are freely surrendered, makes a MOLTEN CALF—either of solid gold, or a gold plated wooden image, fashioned with a sharp metal instrument. Aaron seeks to include the movement within Yahwism, for he builds an ALTAR, and proclaims A FEAST TO THE LORD for the morrow. But Aaron's salvage intention is defeated, for in addition to sacrifice at another altar (cp. 24.3-8) and a covenant meal, the people add orgiastic rites—THEY ROSE UP TO PLAY (cp. Gen. 26.8).

The people confess: THESE ARE YOUR GODS, O ISRAEL, WHO BROUGHT YOU UP OUT OF THE LAND OF EGYPT. The use of the word THESE in reference to a single calf is strange but by no means impossible. The confessional statement also occurs almost verbatim in I Kings 12.28 in reference to calves at Bethel and Dan. Many scholars therefore regard the story in Ex. 32.

1-6 as arising out of the prophetic attack on the worship at Bethel and Dan, and as put back to the Exodus time. This view often carries with it the suggestion that there never was a golden calf incident at Sinai, though this is difficult to sustain.

1. There was an act of apostasy at Sinai. The J version describes this as A GREAT SIN (32.30-32—GODS OF GOLD), and thus confirms an apostasy at Sinai.

2. The apostasy was GODS OF GOLD—this is the minimum formulation.

3. Even if the story is described at points in terms of a later date, the essential fact of the situation remains untouched.

The people prefer Aaron to Moses, Aaron's altar to Moses' altar (24.3), and the calf to the Lord. The form of the image may have been accidental (32.24), or deliberate (4), in which case the calf was either an indigenous Israelite symbol for divine strength (the Mighty One of Jacob), or else a Canaanite element borrowed at a later date. At that later date at least, the bull, like the ark, was the platform for the invisible God.

Many explanations are possible but a minimal historical basis may be postulated. The people under the wrong leader worshipped the wrong God at the wrong altar with the right confession and sacrifice but in a sexual orgy. The serpent in the garden (Gen. 3), the sin at Sinai (Ex. 32), and Satan at the Last Supper (John 13.27) are three illustrations of how sin rears its head amid sacred occasions.

MOSES' INTERCESSION

32.7-14

The real continuation of 32.1-6 is in vv. 15ff., because Moses and Joshua in vv. 18f. are said to speculate concerning the meaning of the noise in the camp. Vv. 7-14 are therefore prob-ably an editorial expansion of rare understanding and insight, a Deuteronomic preacher's account of the interview between God and Moses before the latter's descent, in which the Lord is said to inform Moses of events in the camp. The Lord further proposes to abandon Moses' people, and to treat Moses as if he were an Abraham, i.e. make a new beginning with him, and from him MAKE A GREAT NATION.

11-13. By a reasoned and moving intercession Moses succeeds in preventing the proposed destruction of his people. Moses urges four grounds for compassion: this people is the Lord's people: the Lord has already invested much power and might in the deliverance of this people from Egypt: the Egyptians would mock him if he now rejected his people: fourthly, he is to remember the patriarchs and the promises to them.

14. the LORD repented   I.e., changed his mind, relented.

THE CULPRITS

32.15-24

Moses descends with THE TWO TABLES of stone in his hands. They were small, portable, written on both sides, made by God and either written by God or with divine writing upon them. This emphasis on the tables is important, as will be seen below, and even the Priestly writer has felt it necessary to amplify the words to TABLES OF THE TESTIMONY. Moses rejoins JOSHUA (cp. 24.13), and as they draw nearer to the camp, Joshua says that he thinks there is a struggle in the camp, but Moses in a poetic fragment remarks that he hears not the

sounds of victors or vanquished but rather the sounds of . . .
(it appears that a word is missing, but EVV supply OF SINGING).
The terms of their remarks in vv. 17f. suggest that they are
ignorant of what is going on; but when he discovers what is
happening, Moses in anger destroys the stones, thus symbolically ending the covenant, and then deals with the calf. That he
both BURNT IT and GROUND IT TO POWDER suggests it had a
wooden core with gold plating. The vital point is that when
Moses had strewed the gold powder upon the water (cp. Deut.
9.21 'the brook'), he MADE THE PEOPLE OF ISRAEL DRINK IT. Deuteronomy omits this detail, which does not necessarily conflict
with the present story. If the intention of Deuteronomy, in
having the powder strewed in the brook, was simply to wash
it away, then that is not the intention of the Exodus story.

The people are compelled to drink their sin, but this is done
by way of the test of the ordeal (Num. 5.16-22). The verses
follow in such rapid succession that we tend to forget that they
represent a certain lapse of time and a period of thought and
resolution. Moses had to decide what to do—the first task is
obviously to discover the ringleaders. All the people are guilty
but not equally guilty, and so by recourse to the ordeal, an
attempt is made to discover the chief culprits. As the
sequel in vv. 25-29 shows the attempt was successful. The
drinking is not a means of punishing the people but of testing
them.

AARON is chiefly responsible, but rebuts Moses' accusation
by putting the blame on the people because THEY ARE SET ON
EVIL, and by claiming that the casting of the calf was accidental: 'THERE CAME OUT THIS CALF.' Naivete and mocking
are matched here. The sequel of the conversation is not related
in Exodus, but cp. Deut. 9.20.

FAITHFUL LEVITES

32.25-29 J

Many commentators conclude that these verses are out of their original context, because the revolt and punishment now described seem to differ from the account in the preceding narrative.

In these verses J describes Israel's rebellion in other terms (HAD BROKEN LOOSE) and then shows Moses in action. He bids those ON THE LORD'S SIDE to join him. Moses had already discovered that there were some who had not joined the apostasy, and who more likely than members of his own family, THE SONS OF LEVI, or some of them? In the meantime too the ordeal of drinking (v. 20) had revealed in various ways the most frightened, i.e. the most guilty.

The levitical slaying (vv. 25-29) is thus the direct outcome of the ordeal by drinking (v. 20), because the ordeal identified the guilty. The Levites only killed some of the Israelites. How did they know, apart from the ordeal, who were to be slain, and who were to be preserved? The slain are said to number 3000. Obviously not all the sons of Levi were innocent, for the faithful minority killed the guilty even when it meant THE COST OF HIS SON AND HIS BROTHER. In turn the faithful minority of Levites are now regarded as ORDAINED to the priesthood as the reward of their fidelity.

29. ordained Lit. 'filled your hand', i.e., given, appointed, always of appointing to priesthood. The Hebrew phrase 'fill the hand' could mean: put parts of the sacrifices into the hands of men to show they were appointed to the priestly office; or, to put a man in charge of something, i.e., appoint to office; or, put his dues in his hand, i.e., pay him.

blessing The privilege of priesthood (cp. Deut. 10.8, etc.).

The position is clear. Moses has confronted Aaron. He has
discovered and rewarded a faithful minority, and has sub-
jected the people to an ordeal, and the ringleaders have been
discovered and destroyed. The remainder of the people, who
without being ringleaders are also guilty, are still alive. They
are not to be destroyed (32.14), but they have still not been
punished. Moses now proceeds to deal with the guilty who
are still alive. The narrative reveals both a unity and a progress of events.

MOSES' RENEWED INTERCESSION

32.30-35 J

Moses denounces the people and then, in the noblest passage in the book, intercedes for his people by means of an
intention of vicarious propitiation. Whereas the Lord had
proposed to destroy Israel, and fashion a new people out of
Moses (32.10), Moses proposes his own vicarious death by
which Israel may be forgiven and live. The coherence of the
context of ch. 32 is remarkable. The principle themes are:
Moses' own personal awareness of fellowship with God (24.
15-18; 32.7-14); then the ugly fact of idolatry among the
people (whether Aaron was the instigator or not); the feeling
of guilt and the presence of death among the people; and,
lastly, the intention of either suffering identity with the people,
or even of vicarious substitution for the people, in the leader.
These ideas belong together in religious experience, so that
their religious coherence transcends literary analysis. The
BOOK is a figure to describe those who are at present alive,
and has nothing to do with eternal life. The Lord's reply is
twofold. In v. 33 he refuses Moses' offer, affirming that the
guilty must die, and by implication that the innocent cannot
die for them; but in v. 34 he begins to plan a new arrange-

ment for the guilty who are living. Moses is to lead them to a
known destination and MY ANGEL is to accompany them, but
their punishment is not to be remitted, for I WILL VISIT THEIR
SIN UPON THEM (v. 34).

35. sent a plague   This may refer to the result of the ordeal
(32.20), or it may be a condition of illness additional to v. 34,
or fulfilling in part the threat of that verse.

THE NEW ARRANGEMENTS FOR GUILTY ISRAEL

33.1-23

All J except vv. 7-11 which are E.

Ch. 33 consists of four separate units; vv. 1-6, the arrangements for the departure: vv. 7-11, the tent of meeting: vv. 12-16, the Presence and the people: vv. 17-23, Moses and the glory. These units appear to be unconnected but in all probability they are the detailed working out of 32.34, the judgment on those Israelites who are still alive, and the judgment is departure from Sinai and a living Presence qualified in some way.

EXPULSION FROM HOREB

33.1-6

Commentators divide vv. 1-6 into two or even three portions: vv. 1-3a, promise; vv. 3b-4, the so-called 'hard words'; vv. 5-6, removal of ornaments. Such detailed division is too analytical, for hard words are also present in the phrase in v. 1: THE PEOPLE WHOM YOU HAVE BROUGHT UP (cp. 32.7). The twice mentioned removal of ornaments serves different purposes. The real key to these verses is the question whether we are to understand the passage as a departure from Sinai, as part of the promise, and so the next stage in the inevitable journey to Canaan, or, preferably, as an expulsion—and so the first act of the judgment on Israel at Sinai. On any view vv. 3b-4 are evil tidings, even if parts of vv. 1-2 are 'favourable' Deuteronomic expansions. DEPART means Israel must leave, and they must leave without the Lord: I WILL NOT GO UP

AMONG YOU. Without ornaments, Israel MOURNED, (cp. I Sam.
7.2). V. 5 clearly resumes the punishment theme and fulfils
32.34, but the last clause, THAT I MAY KNOW WHAT TO DO
WITH YOU, are words capable of two interpretations. The
people are to remove their ornaments, and in that state, i.e.,
in sin, the Lord will consider what to do with the people, how
to deal with them. This interpretation clearly contradicts the
context, for the Lord knows exactly what he is going to do
with Israel, and is carrying out his proposals with all speed.
Another translation is equally permissible: NOW REMOVE
YOUR ORNAMENTS IN ORDER THAT I MAY KNOW WHAT I AM TO
MAKE FOR YOU. According to this translation, whether out of
the ornaments or not, something is to be made, and this something would of course be the ark. Commentators often point
out that 33.6 must have originally been followed by a passage
describing the making of the ark, as Deut. 10 shows. Thus to
interpret WHAT I AM TO MAKE as a reference to the ark fits the
context. Israel, about to leave the Mosaic sanctuary at Sinai
(24.3-8), is to be provided with a portable shrine—the ark,
the substitute for the divine Presence of Sinai. On this view
the making of the ark arises out of the Calf incident at Horeb,
and the ark, as a substitute for the accompanying Presence, itself represents an instalment of the punishment accruing to
the people for their fault.

THE TENT OF MEETING

33.7-11

This E passage has the appearance of an independent fragment which interrupts the narrative, except that the neglected
ornaments of 33.6 may have been used to decorate the tent
of meeting. Whereas the tabernacle in P is in the centre of the
camp, is large and served by the priests, E's TENT OF MEETING,

i.e. where God and people meet, is habitually outside the camp, can be pitched by Moses alone, and is served by Joshua. If the ark was constructed in 33.6, then this tent presumably housed the ark. All-important in this passage is the location of the tent OUTSIDE THE CAMP, FAR OFF FROM THE CAMP. This tent outside the camp is to be the place where people SOUGHT THE LORD, and where the communion between the Lord and Moses face to face remains unimpaired, but its place outside the camp is another instalment of Israel's punishment, and fulfils 33.3, I WILL NOT GO UP AMONG YOU (AV: 'in the midst of you'); not that the Lord will not go up; he will go up, but when he goes he will not travel AMONG YOU; he will travel with the people but outside the camp. Thus the tent outside the camp during the wilderness journey is to depict the Lord's displeasure with the wilderness generation and to be a reminder of the golden calf episode.

In this verse two Hebrew words are often left untranslated; if they were translated the second clause of the verse would read: AND PITCH IT for himself OUTSIDE THE CAMP. 'For himself' could, however, and with more reason, be translated 'for it', i.e., 'for the ark'. This translation of v. 7 would then confirm the translation of v. 5b given above, and both together would point to the ark, link the ark and the tent, and confirm that 33.7-11 really continues 33.1-6.

9. the pillar of cloud   This descends to mark the divine Presence; in other words, the tent is to take the place of the Mount in places of intermittent revelation. This E passage is thus not an independent unit, but an integral part of the narrative, and another instalment of the punishment and promise of 32.34.

MOSES' ANXIETY COMPLEX

33.12-16; 34.9; 33.17

In spite of the abrupt beginnings of narration in vv. 12 and
17, continuity is maintained, provided always that the master
theme of departure or expulsion from Sinai is borne in mind.
This master theme, rather than the centrality and significance
of Moses, gives unity to these chapters. (Some dislocation of
the text appears to have occurred. The verses have been re-
arranged in many ways. Probably 33.12-16 resumes 32.34a
and 33.1a. Again, either 33.14-16 must be read to follow 34.9,
or, better, 34.9 should follow 33.13, or even 33.16; 33.17
would be the answer to 34.9.)

Moses is rightly concerned about future arrangements, for
he is about to lead his people into an area beyond his own
geographical knowledge and experience. So Moses complains
that the Lord has not informed him WHOM THOU WILT SEND
WITH ME. Moses enquires the identity of the angel guide promised in 32.34 and 33.2 (and cp. 23.20, 27). Moses invokes
the personal relationship between them—God knows him BY
NAME—and recognizes his favoured position before God, but
these are not enough. He requests particular guidance: SHOW
ME NOW THY WAYS; i.e., 'Make clear to me your plans for the
months ahead as I lead your people onwards.' In reply God
promises two things: First, 'MY PRESENCE WILL GO WITH YOU.'
The Presence, the *panim* (lit. 'face') is to accompany them.
This means one of several possibilities: The Lord has retrac-
ted and will go with them; or he will go, but not in their midst;
or he will be represented by his *panim* as something distin-
guishable from full deity, or as represented by the Ark, or by
a person such as the priest of Midian (Jethro or Reuel, see on
2.18 above and Num. 10.29-32). Secondly, I WILL GIVE YOU
REST, i.e. successful completion of the journey in the occupation of Canaan. In Num. 10.33 the Ark will seek out a resting

place for Israel, and so the implication is that the *panim* is the Ark.

Scholars have long recognized that the sequence of thought in this narrative is very difficult to trace. Within the general exposition just given, a more detailed analysis is also possible. Either on the Mount or in the newly erected tent Moses makes his personal request to the Lord: SHOW ME THY WAYS (v. 13). V. 14 may then be interpreted as God's granting of his request: MY PRESENCE WILL GO WITH YOU. Then we must understand God's ways as God's Presence. V. 15 is then Moses' acceptance and compliance with God's favour.

On the other hand, v. 14 may be the withholding of Moses' request. God says: 'You want to know my ways; well, my Presence will go with you—is that not enough?' Moses then realizes that he is really taking God's Presence for granted. Without it he will not stir from where he is, for God's accompanying *panim* or Presence is the mark that distinguishes Israel from the surrounding peoples. Moses therefore implies that he is not satisfied with God's reply, and his own request still stands. In effect he says: 'I know we have your Presence —even if it is outside the camp—but I want to know your ways—your purposes.' On this view, the assurance that God will grant his request occurs in v. 17 and not in v. 14. Certainly the terms of vv. 12 and 13 recur again in v. 16, where Moses confesses both the necessity of the *panim* for the journey, and also that the presence of the *panim* will distinguish Israel from the peoples that they will meet during their journeys. The Lord's *panim* is thus the uniqueness of Israel. 34.9 and 33.17 sum up the terms of the understanding reached.

Next comes Moses' request in v. 18. This may be the reiteration of the request made at vv. 12.f., and granted in v. 17, but is more probably a new request. Emboldened by his first success, Moses now proffers a second and even more daring request.

THE DARING OF MOSES

33.18-23

The Lord and Moses are still on Sinai. Most things are now clear. They are to leave Sinai; they are to have the divine leader and Presence in the form of the Ark; they are to have an oracle tent of meeting for purposes of divine help and counsel; they are to go to their resting place—to Canaan. Only the question of the broken tables of stones remains unsolved. At the moment of departure, Moses requests a parting present from his God. SHOW ME THY GLORY. Moses begs that his last visit to the mountain be marked by a supreme token of God's mercy—a full manifestation of God's majesty. The LXX interprets the request of Moses in 33.13, 18 differently, and the commentators have many explanations. The view taken here is that these verses are a unity, and that the passage is thus self-explanatory. The threefold beginning to the divine words in vv. 19, 20, 21, AND HE SAID . . . HE SAID. . . . AND THE LORD SAID, are not the proofs of literal disunity, but the marks of emphasis and of narrative art in perhaps the supreme revelatory moment in all the Old Testament. The whole emphasis is concentrated on the words, the statements, the promises of the LORD.

Moses makes the request: SHOW ME THY GLORY. The problem is whether the request was granted or refused by God. Both views are possible.

(a) The request is granted. The Lord promises that his GOODNESS will pass before Moses, that he will proclaim his NAME before Moses and in so doing will preserve his own sovereign rights by withholding the vision of his FACE (*panim*). On this view the GLORY of God is the GOODNESS of God.

(b) The request is refused. The Lord makes his maximum offer (19), the vision of the GOODNESS and the proclamation of the NAME, but *must* preserve his own sovereign rights by with-

holding the vision of the FACE. On this view the GLORY of God
is the FACE (*panim*) of God. This second view is the view preferred in this commentary, and on this view the passage is a
narrative symbolic of the revelation of God not only to Moses
but also to Israel. All through the Book of Exodus, the Presence of God is normally veiled, whether in a cloud, a pillar of
fire, in a mighty hand, in GOODNESS or in a FACE. Not even in
the moment of departure from Sinai, and especially not after
the apostasy of the calf, may the veiled GLORY be shown unveiled.

Nevertheless God offers Moses two privileges by way of
compensation for his refusal. God will pass by before Moses
and during the transit Moses may hear the Lord proclaim his
own NAME, and after the transit shall behold the Back of God,
i.e., his GOODNESS. Whatever can this quite concrete, matter
of fact, but nevertheless quite extraordinary narrative mean?

proclaim . . . his name   The Hebrew idiom means not to call
on the name of, but to call out with the name, i.e., to pronounce the name. God will pronounce his own Name in the
hearing of Moses. Some commentators have found this too
odd to believe. They have assumed that 33.19 is a misunder-
standing of 34.5f. They claim that whereas the Lord is the
subject of DESCENDED IN THE CLOUD it is Moses and not the
Lord who is the subject of the next two verbs—STOOD WITH
HIM THERE AND PROCLAIMED. Similarly 34.6 should be understood as THE LORD PASSED BEFORE HIM AND (MOSES) PRO-
CLAIMED. Nevertheless in the erroneous expansion the strange
conception of the Lord pronouncing his own name persists and
calls for explanation.

you shall see my back   In this passage as in 24.9-11 God appears unveiled. In Ex. 24.9-11 the vision is presumably at
some distance; here God passes by a cleft in a rock in which
Moses stands. God passes by without covering and openly,

but as he does so he will cover Moses with his hand. After God passed by he will remove his hand, and Moses will see the Back of God. God will be seen after he has passed by. The incident poses the question whether man's chief knowledge of God and his mercies are retrospective? (cp. John 14.26) This threefold promise of God's transit, self-proclamation and retrospective unveiling are then fulfilled in 34.1-9.

A FURTHER COVENANT

34.1-35

Vv. 1-28 : J (with some editorial additions); vv. 29-35 : P.

Vv. 5b-9 at least, if not vv. 1-9, are the sequel of 33.17-23,
Vv. 1-5a are concerned with the tables of stone, and vv. 10-28
with a covenant, and are J's account of a covenant at Sinai.
Many claim that these verses originally belonged to the sections in ch. 19 and 24.12-15a and are J's parallel to E's
account of events at the Mount. E's account was preferred,
but now J's account is brought in and, by the addition of such
phrases as LIKE THE FIRST, is made not a parallel account of
events at Sinai, which it originally was, but a sequel in the
form of a second set of tables, and a renewal of the covenant,
broken by the calf-apostasy, in the form of the covenant of
34.10-28.

Deut. 10.1-5 records a second set of tables of stone, and this
may well be the right view. The laws of 34.10-28, whether
conceived as a ritual decalogue of Israelite, Canaanite or preferably Kenite origin, or as parallel to various ritual laws in
the Book of the Covenant in chs. 20-23, are earlier than their
present context. It is also possible to argue, in spite of difficulties, that ch. 34 is a sequel so far as the tables and the theophany are concerned, even if the covenant and laws of the
chapter (vv. 10-28) are originally J's account of the first and
only covenant at Sinai.

SELF-PREDICATION

34.1-9

The commentators who believe that the stones of 34.1 are
the same as those of 32.16 regard the second part of the verse,

LIKE THE FIRST . . . WHICH YOU BROKE, as a Deuteronomic addition. The first stones were supplied, made and written by God. These stones are hewn by Moses but to be written by God, (34.1, but cp. 34.27).

2. Be ready By ritual preparation, cp. 19.11a, though the time is shorter. Moses is now to climb to THE TOP OF THE MOUNTAIN, a summit experience in more senses than one, and there PRESENT himself—the verb is that of 33.21.

3. no man . . . the prohibitions of access are parallel to those in 19.12f. It is only with difficulty or by textual rearrangement that the statement that the Lord proclaimed the Name of the Lord can be avoided.

6. There is no case here for a change of subject for the first two verbs. YHWH PASSED BY BEFORE HIM, AND (YHWH) PROCLAIMED, YHWH, YHWH, A GOD. . . . As suggested, this proclamation of the Name is an act of gracious compensation to Moses for being refused the vision of the GLORY or FACE of God. Instead God proclaims his own Name. In such utterance, invocation or proclamation, various features must be recognized: (a) The speaker—here the Lord is the speaker. (b) What is spoken —here the Lord utters or pronounces his own otherwise ineffable Name. (c) The person addressed. Here but two persons are present. It is manifestly impossible that Moses could have been addressed by or with the Name of YHWH. Of course if Moses had uttered the words, i.e., if he is the subject of the verb PROCLAIMED in 34.5f., then the words of vv. 6f. would be an invocation. Here, however, God is possibly conceived as addressing himself. What this means is not clear, unless the writer was groping towards the idea that God alone hears and comprehends his revelation. In short this event, which is not an oath, a cultic performance, or a piece of crude mythology, is a symbolic narrative to set forth an experience of Moses in the form of the conception of an almost perfect revelation, in which God is the perfect revealer, and the content of the revelation is his Name. The conception falls short of perfection because God is heard but not seen.

8. And Moses made haste This appears to be Moses' first response to the experience described. In vv. 5-7 he is the awed witness, overhearing yet blinded, and in v. 8 the surrendered intercessor, who finally sums up in his prayer the themes of Sinai: God's Presence; Israel's wickedness; Israel the people of the Lord. 34.9 belongs after 33.16.

Vv. 6f. are words of the Lord in revelation which became Israel's words of worship. The Self-predication or Autokerygma by God became the creed, the confession of Israel's faith, and is echoed in later passages (see McNeile). A detailed exegesis is not possible, for the verses are a compendium of Israel's theology of God in his compassionate majesty, and in his majestic mercy. The Lord is always ready to punish but eager, able and abundant to pardon.

A COVENANT AND ITS CONDITIONS

34.10-28

10. Behold, I make a covenant These words probably represent not a second covenant, or the renewal of the former covenant of Ex. 24, but J's parallel account of the first covenant in the form of the ten commandments (34.28). This ritual decalogue may once have contained ten laws, but there are now at least thirteen. The passage exhibits the apodeictic style with additions of various kinds. The covenant will be vested in new marvels yet to be created, and in turn will preclude any COVENANT WITH THE INHABITANTS OF THE LAND or their worship.

13. pillars   Standing stones; ASHERIM are wooden poles; both represent Canaanite deities.

14. no other God   (the OTHER God was ever Israel's chief danger. The prohibition of the alternative was to remain the basic requirement in the Canaanite context in which they would find themselves. JEALOUS is the attitude appropriate to Yahwism in idolatrous situations. Intermarriage (v. 16) specially creates syncretism.

17. molten gods   These must be images of Yahweh rather than other deities. Nothing is said of hewn representations.

24. neither shall any man desire your land   At the three annual festivals all the males are at the sanctuary, and so the land is without defence, but its safety is guaranteed.

28. forty days and forty nights   The period is that already mentioned in 24.18 E. In Deuteronomy Moses spends two periods of this length on the Mount (Deut. 9.18; 10.10).

MOSES' FACE

34.29-35 P

Moses used to hold converse with God and with his people. From his converse with God a reflection of the divine glory used to shine from his face. At first Moses was unaware of this, but later began to cover his shining face with a veil or mask (a priest's mask) when he spoke with the people, for they were frightened. The word for SHONE is similar to the word for horn, and this gave rise in later art to the horned Moses rather than the Moses with the shining face. St Paul in II Cor. 3.7-18 offers another explanation.

THE SEQUEL TO CHS. 25-31

35.1-40.38 P

What was a specification in the terms of divine commands in chs. 25-31, becomes in chs. 35-40 a works report. The report is almost verbatim parallel to the specification, except that future tenses become past tenses and there are some minor alterations, omissions and abridgements, and there are differences also in the order of the contents. A comparison between the Greek text and the Hebrew text of chs. 35-40 shows that there are further differences and omissions as well as differences in the order and in the translation of certain technical terms from the Hebrew.

A good case may also be made for the view that originally the report of the work done consisted only of such passages as 35.4-9, 20f.; 36.2-6; 40.1-2, 34-38, with Lev. 8. The rest of the material are expansions added later by priests who wished to bring the report into line with the specification. Whoever these priests were, they had both chs. 25-29 and the later additions in chs. 30-31 before them, and they assembled their report in reference to the specification. The reader may be referred to the appropriate pages in the commentaries of Driver and McNeile for a full account of the issues just stated.

Why the report of the work in 35-40 should be separated from the specification of that work in 25-31 is not known. The interval may perhaps be best explained by the suggestion that events in Sinai were historically disrupted by some such event as the Calf incident. Then the traditions concerning Sinai including the law giving were put partly before and partly after the Calf story. On the other hand the editor placed the legal sections at Ex. 20 (E Decalogue), 21-23 (Book of the Covenant), 25-31 (Priestly specifications), 34 (J Decalogue) and 35-40 (P's sequel to 25-31).

249

35.1-3. The report puts the HOLY SABBATH at the beginning, whereas in the specification it occurred at the end (31.12-17). A new prohibition, against kindling fire in homes on sabbaths, occurs only here in the Old Testament and is the strictest sabbath law of all.

35.4-36.1. EVERY ABLE MAN (v. 10); ALL WOMEN WHO HAD ABILITY (lit. 'wise of heart', 'skilled') (v. 25). This invitation to the skilled craftsmen is much wider than the statement in 31.6.

18. CORDS are not mentioned in 27.19, which speaks only of pegs. EVERY MAN (v. 23), EVERY ONE (v. 24), ALL WOMEN (v. 25) AND THE LEADERS (v. 27) according to their means and their abilities freely contributed to the Lord for the completion of the work, from hearts both wise and willing.

30. Moses tells the people that God has appointed Bezalel and Oholiab for the work. 31.1-6 did not mention that God had INSPIRED HIM TO TEACH as well as to work himself.

36.2-7. TO COME: lit. 'draw near to God'; work was also worship. So liberal were the people that they provided too much material for the work.

36.8-38. They make the dwelling; the order is from the most holy outwards.

37.1-9. BEZALEL MADE THE ARK; cp. Deut. 10.3: 'So I [Moses] made the ark.'

37.10-24. Next are made the table and lampstand. In the specification (25.10-40) instructions for these three items were given first.

37.25-28. The altar of incense is now constructed along with other main items of furniture. In the specification it appeared in the appendix at 30.1-10.

38.1-20. They construct the forecourt, and begin with the ALTAR OF BURNT OFFERING (so called to distinguish it from the altar of incense), as in 27.1-19. MINISTERING WOMEN are mentioned for the first time at 38.8; cp. I Sam. 2.22. The Heb. is peculiar, and may mean that the women worked in bands. They possibly performed menial duties, or participated in musical rites.

38.21-31. This passage presupposes the census of Num. 1 and the appointment of the Levites in Num. 3f. and must therefore be secondary. This summary statement of the material employed shows considerable quantities of gold, silver and bronze. There is far more silver in proportion to the gold and bronze, and this large amount was derived from the tax and was exclusive of the voluntary contributions of silver. FROM THE OFFERING: the Heb. word is different from that used in 25.3; 30.13 and emphasizes the dedicatory aspect of the gifts.

39.1-32. They make the priestly vestments.

AS THE LORD HAD COMMANDED MOSES—note the sevenfold repetition of this phrase, each occurrence marking the end of a paragraph. It occurs seven times more in the next chapter. Perhaps v. 1a is what is left of a fuller account of the woven materials. Vv. 8-21 record the making of the BREASTPIECE, i.e. the pouch to contain the Urim and Tummim, but these are not mentioned here. On the other hand the HOLY CROWN of v. 30 is not mentioned in 28.36; but cp. 29.6.

39.33-40. The work is now completed, once again all the separate items are listed (cp. 35.11-19). Everything had been done according to the divine instructions, and was now shown to

Moses. He approved it as fulfilling the divine specification, and also in token of that approval BLESSED the people. Approval and blessing likewise recur in the creation story in Gen. 1-2.4.

THE ERECTION OF THE DWELLING

40.1-33.

ON THE FIRST DAY OF THE FIRST MONTH, that is, one year after the Exodus (12.1), nine months after reaching Sinai (19.1), on the first new year's day out of Egypt, they erect the sanctuary and all its contents, and they ordain the priesthood. Virtually three accounts are present; vv. 1-16, instructions for the erection and the anointing: v. 17, a chronological note in the passive tense: vv. 18-33, Moses erects everything for the first time. EVERLASTING PRIESTHOOD, i.e. hereditary in Aaron's family. Vv. 23 and 29 say that Moses had the privilege of performing the first acts of worship, also cp. vv. 31-32.

THE PRESENCE AND THE DWELLING

40.34-38

Moses has finished the task (v. 33) but the CLOUD and GLORY crown the work. They fill the dwelling. This is the theology of the Dwelling, made out of freewill offerings, constructed in absolute obedience and so made worthy of the Tabernacling Presence. In vv. 36-38 is added a rule of guidance for the people. In the descent and the ascent of the cloud, lit up at night by fire, the people saw the signs of their halting and of their marching. They journey according to divine direction. Henceforth in all their journeys the cloud by day and the fire by night witness to the divine Presence in their midst, visible to all the people. Thus the Book ends on a note of confident joy in the glory of the Tabernacling Presence.